The Blind Woodsman

One Man's Journey to Find His Purpose
on the Other Side of Darkness

The Blind
Woodsman

FOX CHAPEL
PUBLISHING

A Moving Memoir by John and Anni Furniss

Paperback ISBN: 978-1-4971-0451-8

The Cataloging-in-Publication Data is on file with the Library of Congress.

Managing Editor: Gretchen Bacon
Acquisitions Editor: Dave Miller
Editors: Joseph Borden, Philip Turner
Designer: Matthew Hartsock
Proofreader: Sherry Vitolo
Cover images by Nolan Calisch.
All photography by Anni Furniss unless otherwise indicated.

To learn more about the other great books from Fox Chapel Publishing, or to find a retailer near you, call toll-free 800-457-9112 or visit us at *www.FoxChapelPublishing.com*.

We are always looking for talented authors. To submit an idea, please send a brief inquiry to acquisitions@foxchapelpublishing.com.

Printed in the United States of America
First printing

Foreword

I've written and played instrumental acoustic guitar music most of my life. Over the years, I've released quite a lot of music, much of which has been used for TV, film, and advertising. With the advent of social media and short-form content, my music found a new home being used as background music for videos. So it was that I learned of John's woodworking. When I first saw one of his videos using my music in the background, I was so moved—not only by his work, but also by the thought and appreciation that had gone into using my music. Shortly after, I saw another video in which John said my music was his background workshop music while working. Truly, there's no greater joy for me than something like that: for my music to be invited into another creator's most sacred space. We quickly developed a friendship that has grown deeper over time. Though I've never met John and Anni in person, I feel like they've been lifelong friends. By the end of this book, I'm sure you'll feel the same.

People don't always remember what you say, but they remember how you make them feel. Art, music, and compassion are some of the best ways to create connection with people. In all they do, John and Anni strive to create this connection, and I think people will remember them for the positivity they've spread, and for how this book made them feel. John and Anni's story is one of love, resilience, creativity, and inspiration, born and nurtured in the heart and expressed through the hands.

Music is more than the sounds emitted when an instrument is played; it's the silence between the notes. So, too, are the pauses in the trek of life. This mindfulness is a big theme in this memoir, and I think it's something many of us struggle with. I've often found myself wishing I could slow time down and truly experience every moment, good and bad, big and small. This is how John often experiences the world. Throughout these pages, you'll see the quiet, important moments he and Anni share, and you will see the impact these have over the whole of their lives.

Neglecting to take these reflective pauses can lead us into darkness, a theme evident in John's story. Moving forward requires vision, which often demands effort and cultivation. John exemplifies this beautifully. His transformation, akin to a wood block reshaped on a lathe or a tree repurposed as an instrument, mirrors how we all can evolve. His journey demonstrates our own potential for transformation.

When John lost his sight, he had to make a pivotal choice: surrender or rebuild. Sometimes, it's in our toughest moments that we start anew, and John serves as a reminder of the potential within us to transform these into our greatest achievements. This won't happen overnight, but if we choose to feel gratitude and find joy in the small things it *can* happen.

This memoir reminds us that we are more than our fears, anxieties, struggles, disabilities, or circumstances. In John's own words, he's not a blind woodworker. Rather, he's a woodworker who is blind. John has known a profound darkness in a way I can only begin to imagine, yet he not only found light in that darkness but has become that light, alongside Anni, for so many others. His story invites us to leave stereotypes behind and see the amazing abilities in people, able-bodied or otherwise, serving to make the world a kinder, better place.

People used to frequently ask if I sang, and I'd answer with a quote: "Where words fail, music speaks." My guitar is my voice. Similarly, John's woodworking and Anni's art are their unique voices, expressing their inner selves. Each piece they create is a captured moment, a chance to reflect and cherish life.

The power of love between two people is also evident throughout these pages. Although their story reads like a fairytale, they are both honest in sharing their pain and struggles, not only in previous relationships but in their own as well. This is powerful and encouraging, giving us hope that we can all build and nurture love. Anni's influence in John's life and work is a beautiful example of partnership in its truest form. What makes them work so well together is their team approach to conflict. It's not about competition or who's wrong and who's right. When faced with a problem, they solve it together, and this has made them stronger in all respects.

John's story reminds us what a gift life can be, or what a gift we can make it. I was moved to tears more than once, simply remembering that truth, one that's easy to take for granted. We all know that we should slow down more often, be more mindful of ourselves and those around us, and enjoy the small things, but it's easier said than done. We need constant reminders, and this memoir is a powerful one.

Whatever your story, you will find connection in John and Anni's journey. This is not a self-help book, but if you are going through something and you feel surrounded by darkness, I can't think of a better example to help shine light on your situation and maybe give you a glimmer of hope for a brighter future. If nothing else, I can guarantee you will feel like you've made some new friends by the end.

What you'll also find here is a celebration of life, as it is. It's about how we always have a choice, no matter how dark the situation may seem or how rocky the road that's led us there. It also shows us how we can appreciate the good times. If there's one unifying message, though, it's that love conquers all. This book is a rallying cry to lead with love, treating others with kindness, empathy, and compassion, and I hope it will help you to find light in your own life and, as John and Anni have, spread that light to others without reservation.

—Alan Gogoll
World-Renowned Solo Acoustic Guitarist

Contents

"Sight and vision are two very different things. Sight helps you see the horizon or the things around you. Vision helps you see beyond the horizons of time and space to create things that never were."

—John Furniss

Photo by Rachel Hunter.

CHAPTER 1

Keys to the Heart

ANNI

Our story sounds made up. But to cite a familiar saying, the truth is often stranger than fiction. In our case, it's better.

In early July of 2012, a friend told me about a volunteer opportunity to paint a piano that would be auctioned for a fundraiser to benefit a local school. She knew I was always looking for something to keep myself busy. Having grown up in Vancouver, Washington, I was very familiar with the school. It was nicknamed "The Piano Hospital" because it was a repair business. It was also unique because the students who attended all had one thing in common: they were blind.

This day, I was painting a small spinet piano, which happened to be blocking the doorway to a classroom. As far as I knew, I was the only person in the whole school other than a couple administrative folks on the other side of the building. I heard some shuffling and looked up to see a tall man with a white cane bump into the side of the piano and place his hand on top of it, smack dab into wet paint I had applied to the instrument. I was a little embarrassed and could tell he was, too.

He held his hand up, smiling and asking, "Did I do much damage?" Luckily, the paint had been drying for a bit, so there wasn't much on his hand. He had a beautiful smile, with big dimples, and his eyes were totally closed.

I apologized and stood up from the floor where I'd been working. Putting my own paint-covered hand out to shake his, I smiled and waited. And then it dawned on me. He couldn't see my hand hovering in the air in anticipation.

So, a little too loudly, I said, "My name is Anni."

Later, the fact that John was working on something called bridle straps when we met felt like kismet to me, a foreshadowing of things to come.

He chuckled. "I'm John. Nice to meet you."

He wiped his hand on his khaki carpenter pants just in case there was paint on it. It's funny to look back, all these years later, and see how this was a perfect meet-cute, like we were starring in our very own rom-com.

"Are you working in here? I can find another space if it's too crowded." I was a little nervous, and my voice shook as I replied.

"No, it's okay, the more the merrier. Would be nice to have some company. It gets a little quiet around here during the summer."

I looked behind me, realizing he had a workstation already set up nearby. John glided past me gracefully, using his white cane to navigate the tight space of the classroom.

"Bridle straps," he said. I didn't reply.

Sensing my confusion, he laughed and said again, "Bridle straps. That's the project I'm working on."

He held up what looked like a dangly, bendy matchstick made of ribbon. It was about three inches long. The thin, white strip appeared to be made of fabric and was capped off with a short, oblong red tip.

"They make it easier to remove and reinstall the action from a piano," he said. He was now sitting on a tall stool by his workstation and trimming the end of each strap with a razor blade.

Later, the fact that John was working on something called *bridle* straps when we met felt like kismet to me, a foreshadowing of things to come. This would be the first of countless serendipitous moments in our relationship.

"You'll have to forgive me. I don't know the first thing about pianos. What is an action?" I asked.

"Think of it as the engine of a piano. It's what makes the whole instrument work." He spun slightly on his stool and pointed across the room. "I think there is an exposed action on a piano over there somewhere, if I'm not mistaken."

He got up and headed to where he'd pointed. I followed him as he made his way to a small piano that was missing a front panel.

"Here, I'll show you," he said.

I stepped up to look at what he'd said was the action, but to me it looked like just a lot of unfamiliar parts. They repeated over and over again in a line, rows of wooden pieces with soft, padded heads on each one.

Standing closely, he reached over in front of me and pushed down on a piano key. He pushed down again on another key. "Do you notice something?" he asked.

I saw one of the wooden pieces moving with each push of a key.

"Wow, that's some impressive engineering," I said.

"Yes, pianos are really intricate machines. They can have up to 11,000 parts, so you can imagine how complicated it can be to repair them."

Continuing and pointing toward one of the pieces resembling a large, padded cotton swab, he said, "This is what's called a hammer. A piano has eighty-eight of these, each one corresponding to the eighty-eight keys. When a key is pushed, the hammer lifts, hitting the string and creating sound."

I always like to say that my hands are my eyes.

"What made you decide to attend piano repair school?" I asked.

"I've always loved working with my hands, and this seemed like a natural next step for me."

He turned his hands upward, showing me his palms.

"Oh, cool!" I immediately noticed a tattoo on his left hand and softly touched his skin where I saw slightly faded ink. The tattoo was of an eye, staring out at me from his palm.

"Yeah, I've had this for twelve years. I always like to say that my hands are my eyes."

To be precise, the tattoo is the Eye of Horus, an ancient Egyptian symbol that represents healing and protection. In retrospect, it was one of the many things that initially attracted me to John. I'd later tell him that, when I first saw it, I could tell he was a bit of a recovering "bad boy," which wasn't necessarily a deterrent. He got it when he was eighteen, partially as an act of rebellion, and partially because he's always loved Egyptian symbology and art, along with their long history and culture. It has become a reminder to himself of how important his hands are to him, as they allow him to see the world and practice his craft. His sharing of the tattoo's meaning on the first day we met was the beginning of my lessons on blindness. I'd never considered how important a blind person's hands are to them until that moment.

After chatting for a bit, John and I got to work on our respective projects on opposite sides of the classroom. "The Piano Hospital," or the Emil Fries School of Piano Technology for the Blind of Vancouver, Washington, had been around since the 1940s. It was a place where blind and low-vision students could learn how to tune pianos and repair the instruments.

The fundraiser I was part of was called "Keys to the City." The idea was that local artists would paint pianos, and they would be placed around the city in public for people in the community to play. The pianos would be sponsored by local businesses, funds from which would benefit the school.

For this project, I'd be working with a group of teens from a local homeless shelter to decorate the piano after I primed it. I'd do the primer, and they would add paper collage elements after it dried. We'd met earlier that week to have a group vote on what the theme of the piano would be. They chose "love" and decided they would each create hearts with poems and drawings that would cover the instrument.

As I was priming the wooden surface, I heard a robotic female voice coming from John's side of the classroom. I looked over and saw him tapping and swiping at the screen of his phone. I listened as the voice from his phone read a list of songs to him. I realized it was an adaptive technology program for the blind. After a couple minutes of more tapping on his phone screen, music began playing softly from the device.

My eyes widened as he turned up the volume. "Big Yellow Taxi" echoed through the classroom, and I heard him softly singing the lyrics as he trimmed the ribbon-like ends of the bridle straps.

"I love Joni!" I said. In fact, Joni Mitchell was my favorite musician.

He smiled. "Me too. Honestly, I think I only know this one song of hers, but it's a great one."

We both started singing in unison as we worked. It felt silly and perfect.

. . . they paved paradise . . . put up a parking lot . . .

As the day went on, he played more of the music on his playlists, and we chatted. I learned he had moved to Vancouver, Washington—my hometown, where I was born and raised—from Utah, where he lived with his parents before moving to the city along the Columbia River in the Pacific Northwest.

John said he had been born in Craig, Colorado, moved to Wyoming as a teenager, and moved several more times after that. The large family relocated often because of his father's job as an electrician in the mining industry. They ended up in Salt Lake City, where he lived for a short while until he ventured off on his own and went back to Colorado. He ended up back in Utah with his folks before making the move farther west to attend the piano school.

For my own part, in addition to being a painter, I was also a photographer and never went anywhere without my camera. I knew the moment I saw John I wanted to photograph him. I decided to take a short break from painting the piano and worked up the nerve to ask if he would mind me photographing him while he worked.

I took out my camera and started snapping some quick shots. I didn't want to distract him from his work too much. I felt a little sad, realizing he wouldn't be able to see the finished photos.

My priming work on the piano was done and I lingered, slowly cleaning up my workspace. I finally got up the courage to ask him if he planned on returning anytime that week. The answer was yes, he'd be there most days.

I gathered my things and wished him a good night and told him I'd probably see him later.

"*See* you later." He grinned widely, and I could tell he made this wholesome joke often.

 C/3

A couple days passed after my first meeting with John. I was excited to go back to the school. While I was, of course, looking forward to continuing my work with the fundraiser, a lot of my excitement stemmed from hoping I'd run into John again.

The kids from the shelter who were going to work on the piano with me were set to show up soon. I shuffled quickly into the school, my arms full of supplies, and saw that a friend had dropped off pizzas for me to share with the teens while they worked. I glanced around, but John was nowhere to be found. I tried not to focus too much on my disappointment and decided to think about how much I was looking forward to spending time with the group of kids I'd grown so fond of. My attention turned toward the faint giggling and murmurs from the teens coming down the hall. Their laughter echoed off the old, tiled walls.

I leapt up from kneeling near the piano and turned around to greet them. My arms stretched out, I exclaimed, "We have pizza!"

A couple of them rushed up to me and gave me fist bumps and high-fives. After a bit of chatter, the kids all grabbed some pizza, taking it with them to just outside the classroom where I'd met John a couple days earlier, and sat cross-legged in a circle as they ate. I was inside the classroom, concentrating on sorting the various decorated hearts they had made. They planned to glue the hearts to the painted surface of the piano, then apply a layer of decoupage over them. Ruminating on their chosen theme, I smiled and wondered again if I'd run into John.

That second day I spent with John hadn't been full of any real conversation. But, combined with the company of the young group and him playing DJ for us, it had been a good day, and one I didn't want to forget.

Then I heard some faint apologies and the sound of people moving around outside the door. I peeked out and there he was, trying to navigate the obstacle course of young adults scattered about the hallway. Good-naturedly, he smiled and said to the kids, "No worries, just watch out for my cane. I wouldn't want to accidentally git you with it." His Western cowboy accent was strong today. It struck me at that moment how old his soul seemed.

I backed up as he approached the doorway to the classroom. "Hello, it's Anni here!" I said.

Turning in my direction, he stopped and stood with his white cane next to him. The cane was almost five feet in height.

"Howdy," he said. "How is your project coming along?"

"Pretty well, the kids are here, as you probably noticed, and they are going to work on decorating the piano today. We'll try to stay out of your way. Sorry about that."

"Oh no, it's okay. I just need my small corner over there and I'm all set."

I walked back out into the hall and saw the kids were finished eating and were getting antsy to start working. We crammed into the classroom, trying not to get in John's way.

He started playing upbeat music from his phone and the teens seemed to appreciate it, joking around with each other as they added hearts to the piano's surface.

Later, after the kids had left, and as I gathered my things to leave, I got up the courage to ask him a question. "There is a sculpture garden nearby with a lot of tactile art in it. Would you want to go check it out with me sometime?"

"Sure, that sounds fun," he said, showing another warm smile. "I haven't gotten to check out the city much since I moved here last year. I've been mostly attending school, or I guess just hanging out with my friends at the apartment building where I live. Here, I'll give you my number."

That second day I spent with John hadn't been full of any real conversation. But, combined with the company of the young group and him playing DJ for us, it had been a good day, and one I didn't want to forget.

✑

A couple days later, I realized I had left a small box of supplies at the school. I took this as an opportunity to go there and possibly run into John again.

My heart was racing when I pulled up to the school. I took a deep breath and put my hand on the front door. It was locked. Oh well, I thought. I'll give them a call this week to schedule a time to retrieve the rest of the supplies.

On my way back home, I felt a surge of bravery and had an overwhelming urge to call John. Resolute, I pulled into the parking lot of a national park along my way. I knew it would be a quiet place where I could gather my thoughts. I parked my car and started dialing John's phone number, which I had written on a piece of scrap paper. After a few rings, he picked up.

"Hi, it's Anni . . . the piano painter," I said. I felt so awkward.

"Oh hi, how's it going?" John said.

"Good, I was wondering if you'd like to hang out tonight?"

There was silence, followed by what sounded like his hand covering the speaker.

"Hey, can I call you back in a little bit?" he asked.

I felt completely deflated, believing this meant he was in no way interested and was just trying to find a good way to let me down. I put the car in gear, pulled out of the parking lot, and drove in silence the rest of the way home.

I was sitting on my couch about an hour later, still feeling a bit sad, when he called me back and asked if I wanted to pick him up and go harvest peas in his community garden plot. It sounded like an activity I'd enjoy, and I quickly agreed!

Later, I learned from John that his hesitant response had been due to the fact that he was short on funds, or as he put it, "broke as a joke." He'd been trying to think of an activity that would cost nothing. If my nerves hadn't gotten the best of me when I'd called, I wouldn't have forgotten to suggest the sculpture garden again, perhaps saving us both a bit of stress. I think, though, it worked out as it should have, as John's garden would become an important part of our story.

⚬⚬

A few hours later, I stood outside of John's door, shaking slightly from nerves. I knocked softly and heard shuffling inside. He opened the door, and I could see it was totally dark inside his apartment.

I was startled by the dim room at first, and then remembered he didn't have the need for light.

"Hey, let me just grab my cane," he said.

"My car is parked right here in front of your place. Do you need me to help you get to the door?"

"I got it, thanks." He found the car with his cane swooping back and forth, and then followed the back of the car, using the trunk as a landmark. He moved around to the front passenger door, where he easily found the handle.

On our way to the garden, my curiosity piqued, and I asked him some questions that had been brewing in my mind.

"Do you mind if I ask about your blindness? I don't want to pry if it's too personal."

"Ask away! I'm used to people asking. It's really no trouble." He smiled, his eyes closed as usual. I thought he looked so peaceful with his eyes closed.

"Okay. Are your eyes shut by choice?" I asked.

"No, I have permanent nerve damage in my eyelids and don't have control over opening them. They are closed all the time because of that. But it's honestly easier for me this way, since I'm totally blind."

"Oh, that was my next question, whether or not you were totally blind. I'm so surprised with how well you get around and how independent you are."

"I'm lucky I have really good spatial awareness, plus I went through mobility and white cane training after I became blind."

I wondered what had caused his blindness, since he had mentioned nerve damage. It felt too early to ask about this, so I refrained. I was hoping there would be plenty more time to get to know him and learn about what had caused his condition.

We pulled up to the abundant community garden, full of greenery. I saw that this was a busy time of day. Couples, families, and solo gardeners dotted the lush landscape. Some wore broad-brimmed hats, some watered their spaces with hoses.

John easily found the garden plot and I shook my head at this, smiling in amazement. There were dozens of patches divided by wooden stakes, but he found his own spot pretty quickly. He told me he shared the plot with a good friend of his, and they were both really interested in gardening.

The peas weren't growing upward on trellises like I was used to seeing. These were growing in a hedge pattern closer to the ground. He had put stakes all around the plot and strung twine around the posts in an almost spiderweb pattern. I noticed the stakes were made of old piano keys. He told me this was a way he was able to differentiate his plot from the others. I could see there was a great bounty of green peas, bouncing on the vine as he felt around the patch. Their little spirals seemed to dance as he patted the greenery, inspecting it with his hands.

I could see that I just needed to jump in and start picking. We had brought some plastic containers, and I laid one near to where he was stooping. I told him it was there so he wouldn't trip on it.

I slipped my sandals off my feet and leaned down to start harvesting. I kept peeking up at him, wondering if his quietness was because he was nervous or if it was just in his nature. I realized I knew very little about him. Later, I would find out that John was very laid back. As in, he was in his own world kind of laid back, and I needn't worry about it. It was just who he was.

Judging from the fact that I had been the one to ask him for his number first, I decided that I needed to be the one to guide our conversation. Honestly, I wasn't very good with silences, which was odd because I wasn't exactly the most talkative person. I could carry on a conversation well enough, but with an introverted nature, I leaned toward the quiet side myself.

This felt different, though. I felt drawn to know him. He intrigued me in a way I couldn't quite pinpoint. I guess the blindness had something to do with it, but it was something else, too. He had a peace about him that I envied. My anxious nature didn't often find the tranquility that appeared to come so naturally to him.

Out of nowhere, he started talking about the pattern of the peas and what had made him decide to try this method of growing them. With his Western drawl, and the way he talked, I was reminded of someone from another era. I pictured him as a farmer in overalls in the 1930s, proudly sharing his gardening secrets with a neighbor. I blushed when I realized I was getting distracted by the daydream and brought my attention back to his demonstration.

I realized John was quite talkative, it just took the right subject.

After a bit, I helped him track down a nearby hose. He watered the pea patch, that same peaceful look on his face.

Though it was perhaps an atypical first date, harvesting peas in John's pea patch was perfect for us, and the site continued to be instrumental in our relationship.

We chatted more about gardening, and after an hour, he suggested we sit in the grass and relax a bit.

John walked toward an open spot on the ground, slightly stooped over with his cane in front of him as he swept his arm back and forth. He looked like a wizard performing a magic spell, and I was tickled with how cute it was. I realized he was making sure there wasn't a shrub or low tree as he sat down. I noticed John had a definitive hump at the top part of his back. Later, we would jokingly call this his "stegosaurus hump," and I would learn it was a result of some serious back injuries he'd accrued over the years.

Cross-legged and sitting on the soft ground, I covered my legs with my skirt and leaned my elbows forward onto my knees. I pulled at the grass, nervously yanking at it and making a little pile of the green blades in front of me.

He pulled out a pack of cigarettes, and I felt a mix of disappointment and nostalgia. I had been a smoker for eighteen years and had quit just the year before, when I was thirty-four. I was worried his smoking might tempt me, but once I smelled the smoke, I knew it wouldn't be an issue. I watched as he held his lighter slowly to the end, careful not to burn himself and trying to feel the end of the cigarette with his other hand. It was fascinating to watch, but I felt myself staring again. I felt my cheeks light up in embarrassment and felt guilty for being grateful he couldn't see me blushing. I both loved and hated the smell of tobacco. It was what John would later tell me he called a "good/bad" smell. That was the perfect descriptor. It was stinky, but in a strangely comforting way.

I built up the courage to ask him something I had wanted to ask since we met that first day.

"I've been wanting to ask you this, but feel silly. Do you even know what I look like?" I laughed awkwardly.

John's grin widened and two heart-melting dimples appeared.

"I don't know exactly what you look like, but if you'd like to tell me, I'd love that. I did ask my friend and she said you are 'one hot mama.'" The friend in question was another artist who was painting a piano at the school, and she'd seen me around there.

Blood rushed to my cheeks, and I giggled at the thought of me being called such a name. I was more librarian than rockstar, but I decided I would take the compliment. I silently thanked this friend of his for the accolades. It was also the moment that I knew we were on a date. No mere friend zone here. Good!

"Well, I'm on the round side, and I wear glasses," I said, thinking it could be helpful to provide more concrete details. "I have gray-blue eyes and light brown hair with reddish tones, and I'm a shorty, only 5'2". I dress a bit like a schoolteacher; I love wearing long skirts and cardigans."

"Oh good, there's more of you to love," he said, referring to the comment in which I alluded to being on the larger side.

My eyes widened, and a goofy grin appeared on my face. Oh, man, this guy was precious.

"Honestly, I had pictured you in a very specific outfit. The first time I met you I imagined you wore a blue dress, like an old-fashioned German dress you'd see in *Heidi* or something."

"Wow, that's quite wholesome! I like it." My grin got even bigger, and my cheeks reddened.

We talked about how much he liked the piano school and what his favorite things about the Pacific Northwest were. He said the school was a life-changing opportunity for him and it was challenging work, which he was grateful for. He said it kept him focused and gave him a sense of purpose. He told me that he'd always loved working with his hands and even had a certification for small-engine repair.

He said his father had started teaching him to work on cars when he was young, which made mechanics a lifelong hobby for him. In my mind, I imagined he could probably change the oil in an engine but didn't think he could do anything more advanced than that. Later, I would be proven very wrong. I soon learned that John was used to people making assumptions and doubting him, which, thankfully, I eventually stopped doing. It was something I wasn't proud of, but I've always been open to learning and letting go of my presumptions.

As he spoke, I noticed some scars on his face, one at his hairline that spanned his entire forehead. The hair along that scar was slightly sparse, it almost looked like he had hair plugs, but I didn't notice this until I was very close. I assumed the hair growth pattern was from whatever had caused the scar. There was also a scar shaped like a lightning bolt on his left temple and a round one on the right temple. I saw some bumps I couldn't quite identify in a couple places above his eyebrows. I held myself back from asking about them. That seemed like a second- or even a third-date-type question.

He went on to tell me about his large family, two sisters and three brothers. John was the baby. I told him about my two sisters, I was the middle kid. I told him I had been born and raised in Washington state. I asked him if he planned on moving back to Salt Lake after graduating from the piano school.

"Oh, definitely not, I plan on staying right here. The moment I got off that plane I knew that I was home. My friend Bud originally told me about the Pacific Northwest, and the way he spoke about it sounded almost magical. I had to check it out for myself."

I was relieved he didn't have plans to leave. I had every intention of staying put in Washington. I had planted my roots, and believed my roots were there for good.

John talked about not being able to see the trees, but still knowing they were there all around. Our area of Washington, like most of the state, was lush with trees. Trees and wood were eventually going to be a huge part of our lives, though I didn't know it yet.

I jokingly told him about a humorous bumper sticker on my car in high school that read "Tree Hugging Dirt Worshipper," and he said that now he knew that the garden date had been the right choice. He said he had a feeling I liked to put my hands in the dirt, and he was right! We were off to a great start.

I thought back something I had written a year earlier, a list of the characteristics of the partner I was wanting to meet. It might sound a little mystical or woo-woo, but I had heard somewhere that writing down your desires was an important part of goal-making.

The number one thing on the list was an artist. I remember adding "woodworker?" in parentheses. I longed to find a partner who understood my own creative inclinations. Art wasn't just a hobby for me; it was a lifestyle. I lived and breathed creative expression.

We started chatting about this a bit, and he mentioned that he had taken a woodworking class in Utah at a school for the blind. You could have knocked me over with a feather. A woodworking class for the blind? I didn't want to sound ignorant, but that was the last thing I expected him to tell me. He went on to share about his teacher, a man named Chris Hathaway. After the class ended, they remained close, and John started working under him, Chris becoming a de facto mentor. Chris was also blind, and one day he asked John if he would be interested in helping him build a woodshop at his home. Up for anything, John eagerly said yes. Chris had been wanting to build a new shop for some time. Working with John in his cramped old shop inspired him to finally start the project. They spent the next four months building a woodshop for Chris from the ground up.

When they were done, they each had much more room, and John was able to utilize the shop to further develop his woodworking skills. He told me of using a lathe and teaching himself some techniques that might be frowned upon in the woodworking world, such as touching the wood blank (a block or piece of wood) while it's spinning on the lathe. "Otherwise, it would look like a blind guy made it," he told me. A lathe works by essentially spinning a piece of attached wood at a high rate of speed. The woodworker presses various cutting tools into the blank as it spins to shape it. It can be a dangerous tool even for sighted workers, and most will advise you to never touch a spinning blank.

I sat there listening to him in awe, unsure of how to respond. Because it was our first date, I was trying to play it cool. But, inside, I was already bursting with love for this man I barely knew. He was, without a doubt, the most interesting person I had ever met.

I would soon learn there was much more to his story.

CHAPTER 2

Walking through the Darkness

— JOHN —

The moment I stepped off the plane, I felt like my soul was home. It was February of 2011, and I was ready for a new start. I'd heard from many people that Vancouver, Washington, was a beautiful city, and I had to take their word for it. Though I couldn't see or smell anything around, I felt a peace that washed over me. I should have been scared, or at least nervous, but I felt neither. I was full of expectation that I felt had been building in me over the previous few years. I was full of hope and possibilities. Anything would be better than the treadmill I'd been stuck on for a long while.

Blindness can do that to you. It can make you feel like the world extends only ten feet in every direction. The smallness of my world felt comfortable most of the time—until the safety of it began suffocating me. The lack of independence took a toll on my mental health most of all, and it also affected my relationships, or lack of them. I yearned for companionship. I longed for a world that felt bigger, a place to stretch my legs both literally and figuratively.

Twelve years before I stepped off that plane in the Pacific Northwest, I had entered a world of darkness.

To be precise, I had been surrounded by darkness long before that. The events that took my eyesight on April 10th, 1998, when I was sixteen years old, made that darkness feel permanent. Initially, becoming blind looked like bleakness, like a loss of my freedom. I've since come to understand

When I focus on the things I'm missing, such as being able to drive, it's easier to be consumed by feelings of regret. Finding my purpose has helped immensely in this regard.

that blindness has saved me in many ways. It has taken me places I never could have imagined.

Now I feel like I was always supposed to be blind.

Though I didn't regret my decision to migrate to the Pacific Northwest, I knew there were challenges I'd face in my new life. Unfortunately, I'd made a lot of bad decisions in my past, and they were still following me to that day. In 2001, at the age of twenty, I'd been found guilty of conspiracy to distribute marijuana. After I violated my probation (more on that later), I received a felony charge. All this to say: finding housing was going to be tricky.

You'd think, as a blind person, I would have been scared trying to learn a new city, but I soon felt like I was in the place I should be, doing the things I should be doing. I've always had an adventurous spirit, and I demonstrated that when I moved to Washington on my own, far away from my family and friends.

Though it was a momentous decision to move, I never really felt scared, though I had plenty of reasons to feel nervous. I was a blind guy moving 900 miles away from anyone I knew. I would be facing a lot of uncertainty, but I figured that was already sort of my reality. In my mobility training, I had been taught how to navigate new places with my white cane. This should be no different.

I could hear the voice of my mom—or Momma, as I call her—in my head everywhere I went, telling me to be careful. With good reason, she was anxious that I could hurt myself. I didn't know a lot of blind people who were doing the things I was doing. Sure, I broke into a cold sweat the first time I used a table saw, but how else was that board going to get cut? I'd lived in Salt Lake City on and off since 1999, and on more than one occasion had walked across eight lanes of traffic, my long legs carrying me swiftly over the crosswalk and just barely making it as the light changed.

I was confident and excited about things to come. When I first heard about the program at the Emil Fries School of Piano Technology for the Blind, it sounded like the perfect fit for me. As someone who had always enjoyed working with my hands, I was eager to enter the program. I hoped getting work wouldn't be too difficult. There wasn't a lot of work for blind mechanics or carpenters. Can you imagine the liability insurance?

The town I grew up in was very small. Blink-and-you-might-miss-it kind of small. With fewer than 9,000 people, Craig, Colorado, was a tight-knit community. If you didn't know everyone, you knew of them.

My dad worked in the mining industry doing electrical work and was known as an expert in his field. His credentials are a mile long, but the short of it is he'd worked for large corporations and was an instrumental part of several mining organizations and certification boards. A childhood friend of mine who worked for the mines (later, as an adult, to be clear) once described my dad as a living legend! With my dad working hard to support our large family of eight, my mom worked just as hard at home to keep the ship afloat. She took care of all of us, cooking and keeping house. On top of keeping our household running, she worked as a bank teller for the early part of my childhood, and later worked at the local job resource center.

I'm not saying Dad didn't do his part, but Mom was a homemaker and did all the cooking, cleaning, and driving—and child labor came in handy, I'm sure. All jokes aside, my mom is the reason I am passionate about baking. As a child, I would sit on the counter in the kitchen and watch as she baked everything from bread to cookies. She taught me how to knead bread dough until it was just right. She also fostered my creative side. She was always doing some creative project. She painted, crocheted, and quilted. She once saved my jeans from my childhood, cut them up, and made a huge quilt out of them—and it's still my favorite quilt to this day!

I have five older siblings and am the baby of the family. My oldest brother was out of the house by the time I turned six, off to start his own adventures, which included going on a Mormon mission to Brazil. My two other brothers also went off to their missions when they turned nineteen. However, I knew early on this was not going to be the direction my life would take. From a fairly early age, I knew I didn't identify with the Mormon faith.

Try as I might, I couldn't commit to the church, and I felt it required more dedication and sacrifice of my true self than I was able to give. The more I felt forced to go to church, the more I grew to resent it. Looking

Though I outwardly appeared to be a normal, happy, smiling kid, I wrestled with feelings of isolation and anxiety throughout my childhood.

back, I think a lot of my teenage rebellion came from this disconnect between who I was and who I was expected to be. I also never really felt I fit in at church, which further exacerbated the feelings of isolation that often plagued me. My philosophical differences with my family came with some tension, but eventually we would come to an understanding (though it took many years).

As a young child, I was silly and quick to smile and goof around. In my adolescence, I started feeling a void. I felt different from others in my family and at school. I was always worried. I worried about getting in trouble with my parents, getting bullied, or not getting good grades. My constant anxiety really affected my self-confidence. To try and fit in, I would say shocking things to get attention, which led to me being disliked, causing me to feel even more out of place among my peers. It was something of a vicious cycle.

Around second or third grade, I had already begun experiencing bullying. I remember often feeling out of place and school in general was really hard for me socially. This continued until I was about fourteen, when I started fighting back.

I didn't have very many friends as a kid, and I was a very timid, passive person. The bullying often took place in the form of intimidation, and I remember feeling scared a lot of the time. Being a sensitive child made me a very easy target. A particular group of kids at school had a reputation for being cruel. They would often pick on me for what seemed like no reason at all. Random threats of violence and name-calling were regular occurrences. It totally zapped my self-confidence, making me feel worthless and insecure. It made me doubt myself and my abilities. I didn't want to go to school or be around other people. I just wanted to hide away. I often felt I would get in trouble for not doing well in school, too, which was hard due to the extreme anxiety I faced there. So sometimes I just wouldn't bring my schoolwork home. Some days, I would pretend to be sick to avoid going so I could stay home and just watch TV in the safety of my home. I would often get lost in my own thoughts and daydreams. And though I didn't have many friends, I enjoyed being alone.

I remember feeling depressed and anxious for most of my young life. I never told my teachers or parents about the bullying, as my passive nature made me secretive, and I would frequently blame myself. If only I could be less awkward and fit in, I thought. I think part of this was to do with me just being different, but I think some had to do with being raised in a somewhat sheltered environment, thus not knowing how to fit in.

Our family was a pretty typical family. We attended church and public school, and participated in extracurricular activities like Boy Scouts. Like most families, we had our problems, but we loved each other first and foremost. My dad took me target shooting, fishing, and for drives on the back roads as a kid. Typical small-town America activities.

While I had my share of struggles in childhood, not all of it was bad, and I have pleasant memories from back then, as well. One of my fondest memories was from when I was about ten years old, circa 1991, when I drove my Papa and Momma up Cedar Mountain. I know I was ten because, by then, I was tall enough to not have to sit on the ammo box to see over the steering wheel any longer. We were still living in Craig at this point, which was nestled at the base of Cedar Mountain. Papa and I often went on drives up the mountain and in the surrounding areas together, which is how he taught me to drive.

The areas Papa and I used to drive in looked straight out of a spaghetti western movie, and Cedar Mountain was no different. It was generally dry, dusty, and sandy. There were sagebrushes and cedar trees everywhere. At the top of the mountain, there was an installation of radio towers surrounded by a chain-link fence. It was basically the only thing up there, other than a bit of a flat spot for maintenance workers to park. Cedar Mountain had the best view of the Craig area. There were a lot of volcanic rocks in the cliffs that created steep, jutting edges. Overlooking Craig and the surrounding areas, it looked like something from another planet. While beautiful, the terrain was monotone in color—beige, tan, brown, olive green, and gray.

Despite being an accomplished, successful person, Papa was a pretty laid-back guy, particularly when we were cruising or target shooting. We'd often chat about science, engineering, or history. Our drives and talks gave me a lifelong passion and interest in all those subjects, especially science and mechanics.

But back to my memory. On this day, Papa was letting me drive up Cedar Mountain. This wasn't too far out of the ordinary, except for one thing—today Momma was with us! Since I'd been driving for a few years at this point, my dad knew I had everything covered. I was able to work the clutch with no problem.

On the other hand, Momma had not been driving with us all those years and was terrified that we would go rolling backward, since the road was incredibly steep. Dad was up front with me. Momma was in the back. Dad was cool as a cucumber, confident that I could handle myself. The road had many switchbacks and steep hills that we had to climb in his 4x4 pickup. Momma was pretty quiet the whole time, as I remember it. It wasn't until we were at the top that I realized she'd been terrified. It was then that Papa said, "I think I will drive down." I'm sure my mom was very relieved!

My dad was the type of person who knew how to do anything. When we'd have our talks about science or engineering or what-have-you, he was always able to explain difficult concepts to me. If something needed to be fixed, he'd do it or learn how to do it and then show me. He taught me to think logically and to look at things from all sides to better understand them. I know now that this memory is one of my favorites because it captures the trust my father had in me. So much of my childhood was filled with anxiety and uncertainty, but having the trust of a man I so greatly admired bolstered my confidence and made me feel important something he did in many ways on many other days.

The holidays and outdoor activities also offered a respite from the not-so-great experiences I had at school and church. Grand Old West Days, which took place every Memorial Day weekend, was Craig's biggest event. The town would shut down one of the main streets for the festivities. It was something I looked forward to each year. There was a rodeo, a parade, and my favorite: the carnival.

Another holiday I really enjoyed was Halloween, which was a big deal in Craig. My church and school celebrated with parties and costumes. I can't recall the exact years, but some of my favorite costumes included Frankenstein, a vampire, and G.I. Joe. Our town was the perfect place for trick or treating. It was small and felt safe. You could walk most places and the whole town would get involved. Think of any movie you've seen revolving around Halloween in a small town—the pumpkins, the decorations, the leaves on the ground. That's pretty much what it was like in Craig, and it was a wonderful experience to have as a kid.

As the seasons turned, winter brought its own set of joys. One of my favorite activities was sledding. There was a big sledding hill in Craig that was popular. The only way to navigate the hill was to have someone drive us in a truck to the top. It was very long and very steep, and known for being dangerous, which gave it an extra thrill for me.

The hill was the back side of a sand rock cliff that overlooked the town. When you were standing on the cliff, you could basically see all of Craig. The town was dotted with trees and houses. The biggest building was a giant Kmart.

Winter also meant it was time for my favorite holidays: Thanksgiving and Christmas. I have fond memories of the food, watching holiday movies, and spending time together with my family. Decorating for Christmas was a big highlight. We used to put a stuffed Santa Claus in a wooden wagon that my grandfather built. I come from a long line of artists, cowboys, and woodworkers.

Snow was a big part of my upbringing. It would not be unusual for me to walk to school in six inches of snow. And yes, it was uphill both ways, as they say. But I loved it. The cold never bothered me, but the heat of summer was unpleasant. It got surprisingly hot there in July and August. The temperature would go from -40 degrees Fahrenheit in the winter months to 100 degrees in the summer. Luckily it was dry and stayed in the 90s most days.

So, times in Craig weren't all bad, and my childhood years there passed in predictable and unpredictable ways as the seasons changed. Still, though, I was something of a lonely kid, and struggled to make lasting and rewarding friendships. I grew up, as kids do, and made some friends along the way. I did a lot of things normal adolescent boys do. When I was around the age of thirteen, for instance, my best friend and I would play video games and listen to music. He actually introduced me to a lot of the music I still listen to today—bands like Tool, The Doors, Nirvana, Primus, and Beck.

I attended East Elementary in my younger years and then Craig Middle School for 5th–7th. I walked to school most of the time. On my way home in elementary school, kids my age would harass me, taunting me with threats of beating me up and calling me names. In middle school/junior high, the school was only about a block away and I didn't experience the same bullying until I actually got to school. The playground was a major spot for this. It was more of the same: name-calling and threats.

During my junior high years, I had a pair of friends who were twin brothers. We enjoyed spending time at the nearby creek and biking through a large grove of trees the locals called "Sherwood Forest." The creek, which flowed alongside the bike paths, provided us with opportunities to catch crawdads. We also explored the trails and attempted daring bike jumps.

These experiences, while good, weren't enough to shake all the negative feelings that had weighed me down most of my childhood. On the day that I attempted to take my own life at age sixteen, I felt like I had run to the end of the line. I thought there was no place left for me in the world and that I had no future to look forward to. In the weeks leading up to that terrible day, I had been thinking more and more about taking this fateful step. My anxiety and depression were at an all-time high. I retreated into my mind, which felt like a prison most days. I was a teenager with no self-awareness or knowledge of what mental illness was. I didn't understand what was going on with me, and I continued spiraling until that day when I made what I thought would be a permanent decision. And it was permanent, just not in the way I had imagined.

A few years earlier, in 1995, my dad had gotten a new job in the mining industry, and we'd moved from Colorado, a state with a population of four million, to Gillette, Wyoming, a state with less than half a million people. There were about the same number of antelope as there were people in the state at the time.

I was thirteen years old when we moved, and I thought being in a new town would be a great opportunity to invent a new persona. It was a starting-over point, a way for me to get away from my junior high bullies and make new friends. Growing up, everyone called me "JJ," but the new version of me would be called by my actual name, John. I thought JJ sounded too juvenile, and I was ready to grow up. I changed my hair, growing it out and parting it down the middle. I wore baggier pants and often sported a band T-shirt. Around this time is when I started having real feelings of rebellion. As I mentioned, I felt resentful of being forced to go to church and participate in a faith that didn't align with me. I wanted to feel that I was in charge of my own life, so I pushed back against my parents' rules.

My new next-door neighbor in Gillette was a rebellious kid, and we became friends pretty quickly. I looked up to him right away, and because he smoked cigarettes, I started the habit, too. Up to that point, my rebellion only went as far as rolling tea leaves in notebook paper with my best friend back in Craig and pretending they were Marlboros. Being raised

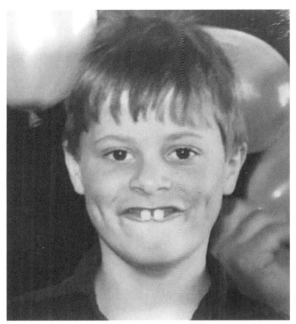

Here I am around ten years old, the same age at which I drove up Cedar Mountain!

in a Mormon family, where even Folgers was considered a gateway drug, smoking felt like a defiant act worthy of a James Dean movie.

While most of my family was busy attending church regularly, I started finding fellowship with other kids my age that were experiencing similar things that I was. It started out with sharing cigarettes and alcohol and eventually evolved into heavier things. Even more than it being an exciting act of rebellion, indulging in these substances and behaviors was an effort at trying to fit in with my peer group. I was creating a world away from home with my buddies that was centered around escape. For me, this was a way to avoid anxiety and depression, which stemmed from feeling like I didn't belong anywhere.

My parents found out about my cigarette smoking fairly quickly. I would often lie and blame the smell on my clothes on having been around my friends' parents, who smoked. But that excuse didn't work very long. My parents were disappointed, but I recall my dad told me he'd also been a rebellious teen.

Self-medicating became a regular coping tool, one I would use for years to come. Being high or drunk made me feel happy and free, and I'd chase these feelings with harder substances later in my life. As time went on, I cared less and less about the things that used to matter to me. My favorite activities revolved around smoking or drinking with my friends. Though I'd always been a sharp kid, my schoolwork suffered. I just didn't care. After a while, I had a constant feeling of wanting to escape my own life.

As an adult, I now realize my parents were doing the best they could and were just being parents. There's something I heard once that I still identify with: From the age of awareness until we are teenagers, our parents know everything. From then until about twenty-five years old, our parents know nothing, and we know everything. And then after that, we realize we're all just people and everyone's doing the best they can with what they know.

But let's admit it, being a teenager is awkward. And I was awkward with a capital *A*. As an adolescent, I was insecure about being shy. I often felt like I didn't have a voice, and I was afraid to speak up. As a result, I overcompensated and would sometimes tell stories with gusto, often exaggerating to make the story more entertaining. I think this was my way of trying to garner attention and feel like I was being heard.

Looking back on this now, I'm a bit embarrassed by my behavior, but I also understand why I did it. I was just a kid who was trying to fit in. And I think my storytelling was my way of trying to connect with others and feel like I belonged. I felt myself being pulled in a darker direction. My choice of music, the way I dressed, and who I hung out with reflected this. I would sometimes fantasize about hurting others and myself. I got into a few scuffles here and there, but nothing too serious. Once, I was visiting my old hometown of Craig from Gillette and decided I wanted to settle the score with one of my former bullies. We arranged a time to meet and wrestled around a bit, but it was pretty much a draw and nothing came of it. I think I was looking for a way to let out my anger and have some agency. Tough guys didn't get bullied, or so I thought.

My parents and I often had arguments about me not attending church services. I knew from a young age I did not see things the same way as my folks, and that was hard on all of us. I now understand how common it is for young adults to explore their own spiritual beliefs, and how this can lead to differences with their parents. In retrospect, I wish I'd had the clarity to create an open dialogue with my parents about my beliefs. But, as a teenage boy, my brain wasn't even fully developed yet. It was such a confusing time.

Though I was raised in a generally very supportive home, when it came to religion, we butted heads a lot. I know this must have been confusing for my parents and siblings, and I know it was for me. As was common in the Mormon religion, boys and girls around the age of eighteen went on what the Church called a mission. I watched as my three brothers went on their missions to other states, even other countries. But I knew this was not for me, and that it was not something that felt right for my life. Some people might say that church was exactly what I needed during this time, but I felt alone and misunderstood by the leaders who were trying to help me.

In retrospect, I wish there had been adults and friends who noticed my struggle more. I don't think my parents really knew how to handle my rebellion, and the harder they pushed, the harder I pushed back. It was like a tug of war. Looking back, both sides could have done better about communicating openly and sharing genuine feelings. With my friends, I think we were all sort of hiding our true feelings about life. There's an awkward stigma around mental health issues, and being a teenager is already a confusing time. Reaching out in either direction back then probably would've felt embarrassing.

Finally, one day, everything came to a head, and I felt like I couldn't handle it anymore. It was April 10th, 1998, and I was sixteen years old.

My older brother was about to get married in Salt Lake City and my parents drove there early. My sister Kellie and I stayed home. The two of us were going to drive together to attend the wedding. I had become so anxious and depressed that the thought of killing myself was a comfort to me. I thought this was a solution that would take care of everything and make it all go away. Of course, suicide is never a good solution, only a permanent one.

After my parents left, I broke into our gun cabinet. It had a padlock on it, so I removed the hinges. This was a few days before my attempt, and I'd not yet resolved to take my life. On the surface, I busted the gun out of the safe just to have a bit of fun with it. I took the .22 pistol with me to hang out with my friend, David. We were going to do some target shooting. I didn't care about getting in trouble at that point. We drove around on dirt roads, randomly shooting fence posts.

As I was shooting at the fence posts, I realized I didn't give a shit anymore about anything. I felt reckless and believed that nothing mattered. This feeling had been building up for a few weeks. I don't remember much about this time period other than feeling very depressed. I felt invisible and that I wasn't getting the support I needed. I often wonder if one of my friends would have noticed and said something to me about the change in me if things would have been different. But as teenagers, we were often feeling the same things, and it was hard to find support among my peers. A couple days after I went out shooting with my friend, I made the decision to end my life.

Content Warning

In the next few paragraphs, I discuss the details of my suicide attempt. For readers who might find this too disturbing, you can pick up reading with the last paragraph of page 44.

When I'd gotten the gun out of the cabinet, I did not consciously have the intention of attempting suicide, though it was probably in the back of my mind. Over the days that my parents were gone, my sister Kellie and I didn't have much to do with each other, so she didn't notice anything I was doing or that anything was wrong. On the day of my attempt, we'd been arguing. Even though she and I have a great relationship now, at the time, things were pretty tumultuous between us. She is a couple years older than me. I'm not sure if our disconnect was a normal brother/sister dynamic, or the result of my rebellion, but what matters is that she saved my life that day.

I don't remember very much about the morning before my attempt. I vaguely recall writing a note, but I don't remember anything that was in it. I think I was in a fugue state. Nothing felt real. It was about time for Kellie and me to leave for the wedding in Salt Lake City, and I had decided what I was going to do. The gun was in my car in the garage, and I had one cigarette that I had bummed from a friend.

We were going to take the truck—the one I'd once driven up Cedar Mountain—to the wedding. Kellie had gone to fill it up with gas so we could leave when she got back. While she was away, I went out to my car and grabbed the cigarette. I walked out to the back porch to watch the sunrise while I smoked for what I thought would be the last time.

I remember thinking to myself, *I'm going to find out what it's like to die.*

I went back into the garage, sat down in my car, and picked up the gun. I put one bullet in the gun. I didn't load the clip; I just put one bullet in the chamber. Then, I sat with the gun in my lap and stared at it for a bit.

Suddenly, almost without thinking, I put the gun to the side of my head and pulled the trigger. It didn't knock me out, but it did disorient me.

Everything instantly went pitch black, and it was painful beyond belief. It felt like a horrible migraine, the worst one I could imagine. I leaned my seat back and then put my head between the seats. I could hear the blood and remembered feeling relieved that I would bleed to death.

I think I went in and out of consciousness, and the next thing I remember was my sister checking my pulse. I just laid there and didn't move. The memories of the next events are more like snapshots from a fever dream: paramedics taking me out of the car and putting me on the garage floor; the pain of them inserting a trachea tube in my throat; me trying to fight them off before being given a sedative. The ambulance ride from our home to Campbell County Memorial Hospital only took a couple of minutes. Once there, the doctor and nurses started stabilizing me, giving me two separate blood transfusions—a total of four pints.

When I came to again, I was in the intensive care unit at the hospital. I don't know exactly how long this was after I shot myself. I think it was the day after or a couple days later. The doctor asked me to open my mouth, and I was able to move my tongue back and forth. I vaguely remember him saying that was a good sign, and then they gave me some pain medicine. I started seeing tie-dye colors in my mind, and I don't remember much of the next week.

Over the next ten days or so, I had intense hallucinations due to the swelling in my brain and from all the pain relievers I was being given. I kept "seeing" myself lying in my hospital bed, which appeared to be next to a pillar in my high school entryway. It was always dark, and I was in my hospital bed.

When the nurse talked to me, I would sometimes "see" myself in my hospital bed but within the restaurant where I worked. Once, when my parents were visiting me, I hallucinated them getting food from the buffet at the very same restaurant. After the brain swelling went down, they started to taper off the painkillers a bit, and I started to come back to reality. It was then that they told me I was going to be blind. Or at least I believe it was the doctor who told me this. I was still heavily medicated, so my memory is muddled.

I remember realizing I would never drive again, never go target shooting, and never run again. The darkness I felt went deeper than my blindness. Despair surrounded every thought I had. Up until that point, I thought my sight was going to return and that my blindness was temporary. I was told that I would most likely not regain my sense of smell, either. My doctor wasn't yet sure if I had brain damage because of everything else happening.

I learned later that the surgery to save my life had been six hours long. I was fortunate that my surgeon was on duty that day. He was an extremely gifted neurosurgeon. He did the long surgery while standing on a sprained ankle.

I am eternally grateful to Kellie for saving my life. I would not be here today if it were not for her quick thinking and actions. I am also grateful to the first responders, nurses, doctors, and the neurosurgeon who provided me with lifesaving care. Without their expertise and dedication, I would have died that day.

Once I was stable enough for transport, I was flown to the Wyoming Regional Medical Center in Casper. Over the next couple weeks, as the brain swelling went down, I came back to full awareness without the hallucinations. It was at that point we realized I had no brain damage. The only lasting damage was that my optic and olfactory nerves, along with most of my sinuses, were destroyed. It was a miracle that this was all that happened to me.

One of the most devastating things to me when they told me I would be blind was that I could not drive anymore. This might seem like such a simple activity to miss, but the memories I made driving with my dad are still some of my most cherished recollections. I'm so grateful for those memories of driving with my father, as they remind me of a time when life was simple and carefree.

As an adult, it's been challenging to lose my independence. I am unable to jump in the car and drive somewhere. I rely on others for my transportation, whether that's a city bus, my wife, or a taxi. There are days I wish I could put my dog in the car and drive to the mountains for a solo hike. Independence is something that I miss very much.

At the time of my suicide attempt, another favorite activity of mine was target shooting. Growing up in the country, this was a common pastime. I took great pride in my precision shooting and had many good memories built around that. Now, it seemed this was another of life's joys I'd no longer get to experience.

I'm so grateful for those memories of driving with my father, as they remind me of a time when life was simple and carefree.

Recovery was hard, as was reintegrating back into "regular" life. One thing that worked in my favor is that I have been blessed with an extremely sharp photographic memory. That helped me very much because I knew all of Gillette and Craig like the back of my hand. Since I had a photographic memory, I could see (in my mind) everything right in front of me. For instance, when navigating my house, I knew exactly what it looked like and where everything was, down to the very last detail.

Some changes were like little stings, for instance the change in the taste of food or not being able to watch my favorite TV shows. I used to watch *Mystery Science Theater 3000*, which is a very visual show, every day. But I just couldn't enjoy it the same way after losing my sight. Back then, my favorite food was strawberries, but I couldn't quite taste them at first. I still can't taste them like I used to. I'd also lost my sense of smell, so it was hard to get used to that.

My adept visual memory also helped me adapt very quickly because when I was performing an action, I could just see the thing, as long as it was something I'd seen before. For example, about one month after I got home from the hospital, I replaced the rear wheel bearings in my old car, completely by myself. I had helped my dad do that job several times growing up. So I knew everything I had to do, and I could just picture it in my mind. Though I couldn't drive my car anymore, my parents let my friends take me out on drives using the car. In a lot of ways, working on the car was my way of coping. I might have felt broken in some ways, but being able to do this one thing that brought me pride and satisfaction was empowering to me. I might not be able to drive cars anymore, but I can still fix them. This is something that helps with my confidence—and gets me out of the occasional sticky situation—to this day.

Eventually, it was time to go back to school. I was going to the same high school, but this time it was a bit different for me. I started working with a mobility and Braille teacher to help me throughout the day. The school gave me an English credit for learning Braille. I was also going to be attending a class for the other blind students at the high school, a Braille and mobility/orientation class.

I excelled in the mobility training, as it came to me naturally. One thing mobility teachers do is make you intentionally get lost so you can work out how to get back on your own. Because I had a crystal-clear image in my mind of everywhere I'd been in school, my teacher couldn't get me lost. Once, she even took me all the way out to the parking lot, and not even that worked!

Mentally, making the shift back to going to school was pretty rough. But I found that learning new things—Braille, mobility training, and generally learning how to do things as a blind person—distracted me for a while. This, of course, couldn't last forever, and I would eventually sink into a depression. But keeping busy helped mitigate that in the beginning.

At first, the thought of using my cane at high school was something I dreaded. It felt like a glaring symbol of my disability and of my suicide attempt. Something that helped me immensely was that my spatial awareness and mobility were very good from the start of my blindness. I feel very fortunate that I picked it up fairly quickly and was able to get around well.

Though I became totally and permanently blind overnight, I didn't need to see to know there was a shadow still following me.

When I went back to school the fall after my attempt, I tried to pick my way down the hallway through crowds of kids. I ended up tripping someone. I was walking down the hallway slowly, at first, to try and feel my way. A kid cut in front of me, and my cane went between his legs and took him out. He fell on the floor, books and papers flying everywhere. His hands slapped the floor and he apologized profusely to me. I realized the collision had bent my cane at the end at a nearly 30-degree angle. I laughed all the way to my next class! Even though the event broke my cane, making it shorter, I still don't feel I got the short end of the stick. At least I stayed on my feet!

When I got to my class, I was trying to bend my cane back to straighten it, and it broke completely in two. My teacher saw me struggling and got to work helping me fix it.

"Here, let me see if I can fix that," I remember him saying.

He grabbed various items from his desk, like some wire, pencil stubs, and athletic tape. He was able to tape it up for me. This is what gave me the idea to splint my cane, and I've had to do this many other times since.

Though I became totally and permanently blind overnight, I didn't need to see to know there was a shadow still following me. The drug use, trouble with the law, and loneliness that would come after my attempt made my world seem even smaller, like a cage I felt I would never escape. But I would find that I was one of the lucky ones. I had a support system that started close to home, with my parents. It just took me a while to acknowledge it.

Looking back on my journey, though, I see clearly now that there were times that I was failed by the very system that was supposed to help me. In the year following my attempt to take my life, I spiraled down emotionally and started doing harder drugs—things like crank, cocaine, and crystal meth. I'd use almost anything to escape my new reality of permanent blindness.

About a year after I became blind, in April of 1999, my parents had me admitted into a behavioral institution. The professionals in the facility were not prepared for a blind patient. While the other kids, all sighted, were having their daily two-hour physical activity time, playing games such as wall ball or basketball, I was told to sit on the sidelines. For my two months there, I sat every day on the floor of the gym while everyone else had free time. I would later find out there was a weight room attached to the gymnasium that I could have been using.

I was also experiencing intense insomnia during this time. My psychiatrist prescribed sleeping medication for me that finally helped me sleep. When I mentioned in a session that the medication gave me hallucinations and that I found them interesting, he took me off it, assuming I was "drug-seeking." This couldn't have been further from the truth at that time. I just wanted to sleep. I was miserable. I found out that they were giving Benadryl to the other children to help them sleep but did not give me any. The aids knew how badly I struggled with insomnia and even relayed this information to my psychiatrist, Dr. Brown. Still, no action was taken to help me. With no opportunity to do physical activities, tiring myself into sleepiness was out of the question.

It was and is my belief that I didn't fit their formula for the types of kids they were treating at the institution. My blindness added an extra layer of complication, and I didn't have the same types of traumas the other kids were dealing with, such as abuse. The professionals there didn't seem to know how to help me cope with my blindness. This might sound paranoid, but I felt singled out and that my doctor had a strong dislike for me. I believe this was why I wasn't listened to. I felt helpless and alone. This led to me feeling angry and let down by the people who were supposed to be helping me. My parents removed me from the institution when they realized that everything I said about my treatment there was true. As an adult looking back on this experience now, I can see just how much the institution failed me, and I was grateful that my parents believed me. To this day, I feel it's important to share this story with others—not because I wish to be viewed as a victim, but because I think it can help others who have ever felt let down by the people who are supposed to be helping them.

The hallucinations continued from there, and I still have them today. I later learned they are from something called Charles Bonnet Syndrome. It is something that can happen to people who lose their sight. It is the brain's way of adjusting to blindness. Sometimes, it can be extremely distressing, but for me it has been helpful. I'm able to layer the lights and colors I "see" in my mind into images. Every room I enter, every object I hold, every person I meet, I also imagine using these hallucinations. I've learned over time to manipulate them.

To put it another way, the hallucinations are similar to snow or static on an old TV screen, but with red and black speckles. It moves very slow, and there are blue geometric patterns that kind of fade in and out like a screen saver. They look like diamonds, stars, squares, triangles, and strangely, Mickey Mouse shapes. I'm able to use this as a sort of background, similar to a wallpaper on a computer screen, that I can visualize an image on top of. While many people have negative experiences with this condition, I've reached a point where I'm not sure what I'd do without it. It allows me to "see" in my own way again.

While I was at the institution, the other kids stole my things, including my clothes. I only had one audiobook I was allowed to listen to for the whole two months, so, needless to say, I was very bored. My time at that institution is something that still sticks with me today, and not in a positive way.

Shortly after my parents pulled me from the institution, we moved to Salt Lake City from Gillette. This was in the summer of 1999, still just a year and some change out from my attempt. I was still acclimating to being blind. I finished high school in Salt Lake City and graduated as part of the class of 2000.

After I graduated from high school, I made a terrible decision and returned to the town I grew up in—good old Craig, Colorado. The main reason I moved back there was so I would be free to do as many drugs as I wanted. Drugs were an escape from the reality of my mind and my life. Self-medicating would continue to be a theme in this period in my life.

To quit drugs would be to lose my coping mechanisms and the only community I had left. My whole life revolved around the next high, the next escape.

I knew the whole town like the back of my hand, so I didn't need to learn a new place. I also knew all the right people to help me do the things I wanted. I had easy access to drugs to support my habit. I was mainly using meth, cocaine, and marijuana.

Marijuana helped me with sleep, pain, and anxiety. But the hard drug use was about escape. Meth and cocaine were often more readily available in Craig, so they were easier to get than weed. The people I did drugs with and bought drugs from became my community. There is a culture and a strange bond that forms among meth users, in particular. Since these were the only people I hung out with, it felt impossible to get away from drugs. To quit drugs would be to lose my coping mechanisms and the only community I had left. My whole life revolved around the next high, the next escape. I think it surprises people to know that I continued using drugs after I became blind. Blindness is often equated with vulnerability, but my stubbornness to live independently fueled a lot of my life in Craig after high school.

I lived in Craig between 2000 and 2003. During this time, I did lots and lots of walking. Most days of the week, I would walk several miles, as much as six or seven on average. That meant I went through quite a few canes. I would wear through a whole plastic cane tip in about one month, and I would usually wear the cane out enough to where it broke about every four months. I had one cane that broke twice. I became very expert at making splints for my canes. All I needed was a wire hanger and some duct tape. I would cut the wire hanger into six pieces, each piece three inches long. Then, I would affix three of these, spaced evenly around the cane, with the first layer of duct tape. After that, I would place the other three tightly against the first three. I would continue wrapping several feet of duct tape up and down the wires to make a splint. It was usually a little bit crooked, but it worked great! The second time it broke was just from wear and tear and the same splinting method was used.

Canes were hard to acquire. In addition to having an extremely limited budget back then, the canes had to be special ordered via mail, which wasn't ideal for something I needed in my day-to-day life. If my cane tip broke, I could not get another one for a long time, so I went through a series of beer caps glued onto the old one. Eventually, I used a large bolt with a half-inch shank sticking out the end of the cane. It worked great, even though it did sharpen to a deadly spearpoint by the time I was done using it. I could have used it as a weapon!

In April of 2001, about a year after I'd graduated high school and returned to Craig, my drug use led to me getting arrested. I was charged with conspiracy to distribute marijuana, which landed me four years of probation. As part of my probation, I had to periodically report to a probation officer and take random drug tests, a fact that will come into play later.

I continued living life as I had and was not treating myself very kindly. To top it off, about a year after my arrest, I broke my back for the first time. Yes, there have been multiple times! This was in February of 2002. Craig gets very snowy and icy, and navigating the icy tundra as a blind person with a white cane can prove a bit of a daring feat. I pulled off some impressive, spontaneous dance moves to stay on my feet sometimes. It's probably the only time I've ever danced gracefully. (In reality, when I try to dance, the best way I can describe it is if all the different parts of my body have become disconnected from each other and start dancing to different songs all at the same time.)

I had just crossed the street and hit a patch of ice. Both of my feet came right out from under me, and I did a seat drop onto the concrete. I heard a big crunch as if I had taken a bite of a carrot, and it knocked the air out of me. I felt a crinkling sensation in my back, too. It took me a little while to catch my breath and get up off the ground. I was going over to a friend's house, so I just kept heading there. When I arrived, I sat down, and my friend gave me a heating pad to put on my back and some ibuprofen to take. That helped quite a bit, so we sat and talked for a while. After that, I went to the hospital because it was starting to hurt again.

The broken back was missed in the first X-ray that they did, and I was told later it was because the swelling blocked the image. A few months later, I was helping my uncle dig dirt when I hurt my back so badly that I had to stay in bed for two days. I went back to the hospital, and they took another X-ray. This is how I discovered the extent of my previous injury. They could see the healed fractures in one of my vertebrae—the T5, which is the fifth one down from where your shoulders meet your neck.

I healed up well enough and continued my self-destructive lifestyle. This led to me violating the terms of my probation when I failed a drug test in October of 2002. That violation is what earned me a felony. It also came with an eleven-day-long stay in the crossbar hotel (a.k.a. jail). Though it was the local county jail, and not a full-blown prison, it was still a frightening experience.

Authorities did not make any accommodations for my disability. While the Americans with Disabilities Act requires that all public facilities, including jails and prisons, provide equal access to people with disabilities, including providing reasonable accommodations for people who are blind, compliance with the ADA can vary from state to state. This was especially true back in 2002. The conversation around inclusivity has improved greatly since then, though there is still quite a way to go.

They took my white cane from me, which made navigating spaces particularly difficult. Luckily, the area I was in was pretty small—I spent most of my time in what's known as a dayroom or pod, an open area with adjoining cells where inmates can interact under guard supervision—and there were no evacuations or fire drills while I was there. As mentioned, Craig is a small town, so when I arrived at the jail, I was relieved that some acquaintances of mine were there, too.

Because a lot of the inmates were in there on drug charges, I knew quite a few of them. We all ran in the same circles. A couple of inmates had been classmates of mine in elementary and middle school. Since I walked all over town every day and was one of the only blind people in Craig, I was fairly well-known and recognizable.

Things kept going downhill after I was released. My drug use went up and up. Most of my money was going toward my cocaine and meth use. The path I was on felt like suicide, only in slow motion this time.

I was living in and out of boarding houses. One I lived in had been in the town for as long as I could remember. When I was a kid, I recall passing the house and thinking it should be condemned. This was a time I was glad to be blind, to avoid seeing the dilapidated building I was occupying. I had a microwave, a stereo, a bed, and a nightstand.

Because I wasn't taking very good care of myself, I ended up getting a life-threatening sinus infection. It was easy to ignore the signs of illness when I was in a continual state of intoxication. My life felt like a dream most days, and not the good kind.

I ended up in the hospital. Even though those were some of my darkest days, being hospitalized was a relief from wandering aimlessly through my life. I felt taken care of by the staff and appreciated the stability of having good food and eating a balanced diet.

Let's just say I was not the picture of health. My blindness and mental health challenges made it difficult to manage my own care. I had been living on hard-boiled eggs and cups of noodles when I did eat. I was rail thin and so skinny that my clothes hung off me. Nobody really said anything to me about my appearance until a neighbor commented one day that my eye looked swollen and red. This is what prompted me to go get checked out by a doctor.

When I'd shot myself in the temple, most of my major sinuses were destroyed, including the natural drainage path. My sinuses could not flow as they should. I first noticed the infection in January of 2003, nearly five years after my attempt. The years of drug use and abuse to my body created the perfect environment for an out-of-control infection to take hold. While I wasn't snorting anything—instead, I smoked or injected—my immune system was very weak. After my attempt, I was instructed by doctors to never blow my nose because of the damage that had been done. I could injure myself if I blew too hard, so the infection I developed had the perfect place to sit and grow out of control. It was one of the worst my doctors had seen, and they didn't understand how I'd even survived long enough for them to examine me.

Initially when I began to feel sick, I went to a doctor who ordered a CT scan of my skull. It showed that I had a large abscess formed from the raging infection, and it was right next to my brain. They wasted no time telling me I would need surgery. I was flown by jet to the Denver airport and then by helicopter to the hospital. That was when I realized how serious the situation was.

I was fortunate to make it out of the Denver hospital alive. The conditions I was exposed to in the room where I recovered were less than ideal. I was in the same room as two people who both had severely communicable infections, including but not limited to tuberculosis. There were dozens of used disposable thermometer covers on the windowsill. We all shared the same single bathroom. I have been in roadside rest stops that were cleaner than the room we were sharing. My shoes stuck to the bathroom floor even after they finally cleaned it. I must have had many angels protecting me.

The surgery they performed on me was done by an intern, which I did not know until after the fact. The reconstruction of my skull and face were poor, to say the least. They did not get rid of the infection, and I contracted another bacterial infection on top of the one I already had.

The infection came back with a vengeance. About a month and a half later, in March of 2003, I was stupidly still using meth, which didn't help my situation much. When it came back, it got so out of control that it severely infected the bone of my forehead and another large abscess appeared right next to my brain. This was a recipe for something much bigger and more aggressive.

Since my sinuses had been destroyed by the gunshot, all I had between my brain and the abscess was scar tissue and a very tough but very thin layer of what's called fascia. This is a material that covers the muscles in your body, and that is what they used to support my brain after I shot myself. Because the sinuses that were destroyed had made up the front of the braincase in my head, they had to put something in its place during the emergency surgery after my suicide attempt. The best option at the time was some fascia and muscle from my own right leg. That was now the tenuous barrier between my brain and the abscess.

The infection in the bone had gotten so bad that my head had swollen considerably. This was another time I must have had a whole host of divine beings protecting me. The doctors that performed my second surgery told me they agreed. I do not know how I was still alive without permanent brain damage, at the very least. They said any other time they had seen a sinus infection that was as severe as mine, the patient did not live. Despite the severity of my condition, the surgeons were finally able to completely eradicate all the infections.

They reconstructed a drainage path that now works so well that I have never had a sinus infection since (knock on wood). The bone had gotten so infected that it could not be put back and had to be disposed of. I was without a forehead bone for eighteen months after this, until I could handle reconstructive surgery.

My parents came to pick me up at the hospital and bring me back to their home in Salt Lake City to recover and try to get my life back on track. I had to take antibiotics via an IV for six weeks. I was in pretty rough shape. All the bone from my eyebrows to my hairline, and from temple to temple, was missing. All I had was part of my face to cover that area for the next eighteen months while my body healed enough to safely accept a prosthetic plate to replace the bone I had lost to the infection.

Many people might think that this was the critical turning point in my life that finally led me to get clean. This event *did* really start me down the road toward healing, but it wasn't the last time I'd find myself on the wrong side of the law. In November of 2003, just eight months after being released from the hospital, I violated my probation again by failing another drug test, and I was incarcerated a second time. The authorities sent me back to the jail in Craig. A lot of the same guys were still in there, and they made me feel welcome by pounding on the pod windows and cheering for me. It was like something you'd see in a movie, but this wasn't the kind of movie I necessarily wanted to star in.

This time, I was in for forty-five days, and it wasn't long before I was back out in Craig, in trouble once again. I fell into my old habits and started hanging with the same people. I started using meth and cocaine again, but fortunately this would be the last time before I quit for good. I'm not proud of these times, with patterns of behavior I repeated over and over again. I'm not sure why I was given so many chances, but I did eventually wake up and make the changes in my life that I needed to.

It might sound like my life back then was full of darkness and desperation, and it was, but it also had its bright spots. In 2002, two years after I'd moved back to Craig, I met my best friend, Bluford "Bud" Dotson. I was introduced to him by a friend of mine, his nephew, Chris. He thought we would be kindred spirits because we shared so many interests, and he was right. We both had a love for cooking, music, movies, nature, and animals, and we shared similar worldviews.

People have often told me that I am an old soul and that I am, at heart, an old man. I think my friendship with Bud proves this. Bud was thirty-nine years my senior, but we quickly became friends. He and I were so alike that he said I was born thirty years later than I should have been.

Unlike most of the friends I've made since becoming blind, I had the good fortune of actually seeing Bud once. I was around ten years old, and I was riding by his house on my bicycle. He was standing in his driveway smoking a cigarette, and I remember thinking that he didn't seem to fit in with the folks of Craig. He was short and had on a colorful knit hat. He was wearing a hemp necklace, and he had bright, white hair. As I rode by, I said, "Smoking is bad for you." Bud returned with an expletive to let me know I could mind my own business next time. It's funny to me that we'd become friends these many years later.

He was my savior while I was in Craig because he didn't do hard drugs. He was my safe place away from the chaos that was the rest of my life. Bud did not judge me for my habits; he would take me in when I needed to get away from all the wrong places and dangerous situations I put myself in. Since I knew some "colorful characters," I made sure that no one knew

Bud's friendship saved my life, and he offered me a place for peace in an otherwise chaotic time.

where Bud lived. I needed a place where nobody could find me, away from all the bad influences.

Being at Bud's made me feel normal. We would make stew, bake cookies, drink coffee, and "watch" movies. Bud had an extensive movie collection and I still enjoy the same movies over and over again today. Some favorites included *Spies Like Us*, *Young Frankenstein*, *The Long Kiss Goodnight*, *Shrek*, *Blazing Saddles*, the early *Star Wars* movies, and *The Lord of the Rings* trilogy.

We loved going on long walks and just talking about anything and everything. One time, we went fishing together and didn't catch anything but a sunburn. Still, it was nice to spend the time with him. Our time together was quiet and allowed me to slow down.

Bud loved animals and had two cats, Clyde and Jenny. He also had four doves, and one of the birds loved to box. They were free to come and go as they pleased, flying around his place during the day.

Bud lived in a single-wide trailer. He had a collection of this and that—a lime-green transparent Jesus bust, shark teeth, old collectibles. He even hung one of my Frankenstein canes on his wall in memory of all the walks we went on and the times we had hung out together. He was a man rich with stories and personality.

I know that Bud was brought into my life for a reason. He truly saved my life. He taught me many things that have served me well. His love of nature and deep gratitude for living things were a reminder to me to value my own life. He had a profound love for Washington State, and he told me many stories about the piece of land he'd owned out on the peninsula near the rainforest. He'd grown up in Craig, then moved to Washington for a while after hitchhiking all over the country for many years. He went all the way to Washington from Florida, then back again. After losing his place in Washington, he'd moved back to Craig. His stories of that area gave me a love of the state, and I always hoped to make my way out there. Little did I know at the time that I eventually would.

I credit Bud with providing me a space to be myself, something I was often denied in my life, and his friendship paved the way to my recovery, though it wouldn't come immediately. Bud was always optimistic, even in the face of hardship. He has since passed from esophageal cancer, and I miss him greatly. In typical Bud fashion, though, the day he'd told me he had cancer, he'd said, "I haven't been able to eat anything for over a week and have had heartburn. They put a scope down my throat and there is a big patch where it is coal black. But other than that, I'm okay." With Bud, tomorrow would always be better. This is an attitude that has helped me immensely throughout my life.

Back in those days, though, I had no idea how I would ever get out of Craig. It seemed out of reach, like a pipe dream. I lived on social security supplemental income, and I had no job prospects of any kind. I had no idea where to start, and I thought I would always have to rely on my benefits. I believed I would never have truly gainful employment. I had a few things stacked against me—such as being a blind felon with no work history.

There are certain jobs that are common for people who are blind. A few that come to mind are software engineers, massage therapists, teachers, lawyers, and customer service representatives. I had briefly considered massage therapy, but the other jobs seemed completely out of my wheelhouse. On top of that, I didn't have much in the way of computer skills.

I've always been a hands-on type of guy. I grew up helping my papa fix our cars, work on plumbing, or with whatever else he might be doing around the house. He gave me a deep love of science, mechanics, and craftsmanship of all kinds. I knew I would have been miserable sitting at a computer all day.

Finding employment with a disability is difficult in general. The unemployment rate for blind people is upwards of seventy percent according to The World Services for the Blind.[1] This is due to a combination of factors: lack of transportation, no accommodations or accessibility in the workplace itself, and, lastly, outdated ideas about what blind people are capable of. These workplace barriers make it extremely difficult to find employment.

Even after becoming blind, I am still far better at working with my hands than I am at anything technology-based—not to mention it brings me way more satisfaction. I could still work on cars because I had helped my dad when I was growing up. With my still very visual memory, I could see every step in my mind. But my passion for mechanics and workmanship turned out to be a stumbling block, not a stepping stone. Those kinds of industries are inherently dangerous, and there was no way I could get hired for a regular job doing any of the things I am most skilled at. Most employers in these industries would view me as a liability due to my blindness. Self-employment at this time wasn't an option. I didn't have the resources or any idea where to start. I'd barely had a job in my life, let alone developed the tools necessary to run my own business.

With seemingly no prospects, the focus of my life during my years in Craig was on drugs. I was lost in so many ways: emotionally, mentally, and spiritually. Finally, in 2003, after the recurrence of the infection and the second surgery, I knew if I did not change my ways, I was going to die.

It was then that I swallowed my pride and reached out to ask for help from my parents. I would most likely not be alive today without their

Lee Rogers, "Employment Barriers for the Blind and Visually Impaired," World Services for the Blind blog (June 16, 2021), https://www.wsblind.org/blog/2021/6/16/employment-barriers-for-the-blind-and-visually-impaired.

support. At the time, they weren't in my life much, and this was mostly due to me pushing them away. But when I called, they came immediately.

I can't mention the various saviors in my life without mentioning my parents and my family in general. Although we have, shall I say, fundamental differences in religious philosophy, they never turned their back on me. This includes my extended family. For example, when I first moved back to Craig in 2000, my aunt and uncle often helped me with groceries. After my first arrest in 2001, they took me in when I needed shelter. There were many times throughout my late teens and early twenties when I was couch-surfing and essentially homeless. I'm grateful to all those who gave me a helping hand.

But, even with this support system, getting my life on the straight and narrow wasn't a fast process. As I mentioned earlier, after I was released from the jail in Craig for the second time in 2003, I quickly fell back into some of my old habits of drug abuse. Since I'd failed my drug test due to meth use, this time I was given a court order to clean up my act, or I would go to state prison for two years. I was also told I'd be given another felony charge.

In spring of 2004, I entered a drug rehab center in Grand Junction, Colorado. To be honest, I had no real desire to get clean, but potential prison time was a great motivator. I spent two months there. Even though it was 200 miles away from Craig, I knew people at the rehab center. Luckily, I didn't have to go through physical detox. Most of what I experienced was emotional. Letting go of drugs as my main coping mechanism was like a grieving process. Losing my sight had been difficult, to say the least, and drugs made it easier to cope with the loss. Without them, I was just stuck facing my blindness. The two months I was in rehab gave me the space to face down some of those initial hard things and sort of get a head start on my recovery, without drugs available to help distract me. While there, I went to group therapy, listened to books, and formed friendships. These were all helpful tools to have at the time.

After rehab, I reached out to my parents again, and again they brought me back to their home, where I started the real business of recovery. As I said, the threat of prison was what got me to finally kick myself in the butt and clean up my act. It was important that I get out of Craig so I could get away from the trouble I had been wrapped up in.

The following two years were some of the hardest of my life, but through my own stubborn will and the support of all those around me, I was able to once and for all get off meth, cocaine, and probation. During those two years, I kept myself occupied with audiobooks from the Library of Congress, and I listened to a lot of music.

Because I was struggling with depression, my doctors put me on various antidepressants. Some of them worked, some didn't. I had severe insomnia, so bad that I wouldn't sleep for days sometimes. I would only get two to three hours of sleep per night on average. I hated hearing the birds in the morning because it meant that I had been up all night again and had to face the day exhausted. Eventually they put me on an antipsychotic medication, Seroquel, that was one of the only things that made me sleep. It ended up causing permanent damage to my body in many different ways. I gained seventy pounds in a matter of months, and it caused intense digestive problems. I'm still recovering from the lasting effects but no longer have to take it. The withdrawal was 1,000 times worse than any withdrawal from hard drugs that I experienced. The first year after I stopped taking it, I had nausea constantly and felt like I had the flu.

I've had to come around to the reality that I'll always have insomnia and I've found ways to deal with it. I sleep more now and struggle less with depression with the help of natural medicine and mental exercises. I'm also more active now, so working myself into exhaustion is a relief to me because it means I'll get a full night's sleep.

On one of my darkest nights I wrote a poem about my insomnia:

> *Trapped in the prison of my room*
> *Jailed by the night*
> *Waiting . . . waiting . . . waiting*
> *For the dawn to come release me*

Meditation became a helpful tool in managing my insomnia. And eventually the long hours spent in the woodshop helped me feel tired at the end of each workday. Getting over my sleep deprivation was a major milestone in my recovery from hard drugs and in my mental health journey. It's incredible what a lack of sleep can do to someone's perception of the world.

After getting clean, the sun started peeking through the clouds, and I felt I was at last ready for the next step of really taking ownership over my life. My mental health is something I still struggle with, but in healthier ways. Some days, I can forgive myself. Some days, I can't. It's easy to forgive myself when I'm celebrating my triumphs. When I focus on the things I'm missing, such as being able to drive, it's easier to be consumed by feelings of regret. Finding my purpose has helped immensely in this regard.

CHAPTER 3

Losing Sight, Gaining Vision

— JOHN —

In 2004, hope came in the form of a new piece of hardware, so to speak.

My time came to have my new "hood" installed—a.k.a. my prosthetic forehead. I like to say they installed some new siding and patched the drywall as they rebuilt my forehead. I am fortunate not to have many visible scars from any of my surgeries.

For the prosthetic plate, they first took a special kind of CT scan. They sent the images to a company that created the plate out of carbon fiber. My doctor said it fit like a puzzle piece. The surgery to install it was only a couple hours long, and I was back home in a few days. I felt like Humpty Dumpty, being put back together again, a welcome experience after all the coming apart I'd had throughout my life.

About a year later, I decided it was time to start trying to get a job and really begin my life. I contacted Utah's Division of Services for the Blind and Visually Impaired, which was a branch of vocational rehab in Salt Lake City. This was a state-funded program that gave people access to resources to help them get training and jobs. It's not a drug or physical rehab. Here, I could get training in various fields and have access to adaptive equipment. Part of their program was a two-month independent living course in which clients would learn what they needed to know to successfully live independently.

They required it because their clients were usually young adults transitioning from living with their parents to living on their own. There were also newly blind adults who utilized the program and needed to learn

It was woodworking that brought me to piano work, and it was piano work that brought me to my new life, and eventually, my love.

the same things, such as cooking and cleaning, computer skills, and braille, plus mobility and navigation skills.

The program took place at a school that offered a woodworking class, and to be honest, I thought this was a little wild. Blind people with power tools? But because of my adventurous spirit, I knew I wanted to at least give it a try. Little did I know that I would find my passion and future profession there, but not at all in the way I imagined.

I am an odd duck because I frequently do things that blind people are not typically known to do. The program managers I worked with did not quite know what to do with me because of my unique interests. This was the case with vocational rehab as well. However, in late 2005, I signed up for the woodworking class, and I found that I had an innate understanding of the craft right from the start. I knew I had found something I was deeply passionate about, and it lit a fire in me.

It was here that I met Chris Hathaway. He was the teacher of the woodworking class, and we became fast, close friends. Chris had been the woodworking teacher at the school for about ten years. He was legally blind, with a small amount of vision in one of his eyes. Without him, one of the most significant parts of my story would never have happened. He is by far one of the best teachers I've ever met. He had an intuitive ability to read the students and show them how to reach their potential. He taught the students not just to be a woodworker who is blind, but to be a fine woodworker who is a quality craftsperson, despite blindness.

The quality of the pieces that were built in that shop class was beautiful, from my perspective. I could feel that the joinery was perfect, and from the descriptions that others gave me, I could tell they agreed. People built furniture, bookshelves, dinner tables, TV tables, you name it. It was remarkable, and it expanded my appreciation for other people facing blindness.

He taught us to use various types of wood and to utilize the vibrant colors and varying grain patterns. He encouraged us to use clear coat finishes because it makes the wood display its colors and grain patterns nicely. He was particularly picky about finishing work, i.e., sanding and applying a clear coat. This was a cumbersome process, but I learned quickly not to skip or rush any steps.

I also learned that if you don't spend the right kind of effort and time, the finished piece won't look nearly as good as you want it to. If you want to be a woodworker, particularly a fine woodworker, you must be patient, or you might as well just give up. The sanding alone will drive you out of your mind, because you sand until you think your arm will fall off, then you sand until you think your other arm will fall off, and then you're maybe just a third of the way done.

The first project I made was a simple jewelry box. It was made of purpleheart, a deep maroon hardwood from Central and South America. The boards had to be cut into smaller pieces, which meant I had to learn how to use a table saw for the first time. Even though I had an adventurous spirit, I knew enough to have a respectful amount of fear for the tool. It was a dangerous and scary piece of equipment, and I was mildly terrified the first time I used it.

Being scared of power tools can be dangerous, though. The first time I used the table saw, I had to prepare myself and give myself a pep talk. I said to myself, "You know what you're doing. You can do this. Follow the safety rules, and you'll be just fine."

Then I set up my measurements using a Click Rule—a tactile measuring device I'll discuss a little more later. Using the Click Rule, I measured the distance I needed between the saw blade and the movable part of the saw called the fence. A fence locks down and is a guide to help make straight cuts at exact dimensions on a piece of wood. I then felt the distance I had between the blade and the fence so I could gauge where to position my hands to safely cut the piece of wood.

I moved the board into position up against the fence in front of the saw blade, gathered my courage, and flipped the switch.

Though my hands were shaking, I held my grip firm and trusted that my preparations would keep me safe. (It took many years before I stopped getting the shakes at the thought of using the table saw.) The sound the blade emitted was intense: a whirring scream. Most of the time, woodworkers use hearing protection because of this. The sounds of the saw can be every bit as intimidating as the fear of injury. At first, I didn't feel safe using hearing protection because I felt like I needed every sense I had left. In a way, I felt that I needed my hearing to "see" better. I felt like it would be obstructing my "vision" in some strange way. You don't put sunglasses on when you're in an operating room, after all! Nowadays, I do use hearing protection.

As I mentioned, I originally used a device called a Click Rule to measure. I now use something called a Rotomatic, which I will explain later. The Click Rule is a tactile measuring tool for people who are blind or have low vision. It is a metal shank with grooves machined in the sides at every one-sixteenth of an inch. There is a tab on the top of the shank every one-half inch. This is mounted inside of a housing with a ratchet mechanism that gives one click per one-sixteenth of an inch when extending the calibrated measuring device out of the body of the ratchet mechanism.

I also used something called a biscuit cutter, also known as a biscuit plate joiner. It was my first time using this small but potentially dangerous piece of machinery. It's a woodworking tool that is used to join two pieces of wood together. It does this by cutting a small, crescent-shaped hole in the edge of each piece of wood, and then inserting a biscuit (a small, oblong piece of wood) into the holes. The biscuits are then glued in place, and the joint is clamped together. When the glue dries, the biscuits create a strong and secure joint.

As I was building the jewelry box, I felt very confident, but I knew it wasn't perfect. The lid was crooked, and the seams weren't as clean as I would have liked them to be. But it wasn't bad for a first project, especially one made by a blind guy.

My first big project in the class was a rifle case made of purpleheart wood with a strip of Padauk on the front and back of the lid. I made it so I could store my collection of black powder muzzleloaders. The case was basically just a bigger version of the jewelry box, except for the addition of a lock and latches. The hinge was a type called a piano hinge, which had about thirty screws. By the time I was done installing the hinge, I had an open wound on the palm of my hand from a large blister. This was caused by repetitive use of the screwdriver. Ouch! Needless to say, my hands are much tougher now. One of my blind friends thought I had leather gloves on one time because my hands are so calloused.

I immediately fell in love with woodworking. It appealed to my scientific nature, and with my keen visual imagination, I was easily able to plan out designs in my mind. Woodworking gave me a healthy focus. I was making furniture instead of making bad decisions. It motivated me with a renewed sense of purpose, and I had hope for the first time in a long while.

I really felt like I had found my "thing." It felt like a gift I had been born with, though it took me years to discover I had it. I hoped to make a career in the field. But how?

While attending the school, and after a couple of months of trying to find a job to fit my skills, I saw the writing on the wall, as the saying goes. I realized my dream was not really going anywhere. Who was going to hire a blind woodworker? I still wanted to continue my woodworking as a hobby, however. About a year after I started the woodworking class, Chris retired from teaching and since things were going nowhere with my vocational rehab, he invited me to work with him in his workshop at home.

Chris and I hit it off right away. He recognized potential in me, and we had a lot in common. We clicked immediately, bonding over our shared love of movies, music, and food. We were kindred spirits, united by our shared passions.

Woodworking gave me a healthy focus. I was making furniture instead of making bad decisions.

Making friends has never been easy for me, especially after I became blind. Trying to find a social life as a blind person can be incredibly isolating. People often don't know how to approach me, and I can't see them, so it's hard for me to make conversation with them. This can lead to feelings of loneliness and frustration.

People may be afraid to walk up to a person that is blind because they don't know how to interact with them. They may worry about saying the wrong thing or offending the person. And on the other side, blind people can't see the facial expressions or body language of others, which can make it difficult to read social cues. This can make it hard to know if someone is interested in being friends or if they are just being polite.

Participating in activities that sighted people take for granted—such as going to an event or party—can be difficult, too. This can make it harder to meet new people and make friends. And in my experience, since I am totally blind, generally the only way I know that a person is in a given room is if they are talking to someone else. This can prove challenging in that I don't want to interrupt them or make an already awkward situation even more awkward.

Most of the time, the only reason a stranger approaches me is to ask if I need help. This is always appreciated; however, it would be nice if someone came up to just say "hi." I would love to be treated like an equal versus assuming I am helpless or lost.

I think there is a romanticizing of blindness that happens in our society. We are just people like anyone else, minus one of our senses. For example, one time I was standing outside of an outpatient rehab center for court-ordered rehab, and I was smoking a cigarette while waiting to go into my therapy meeting. A passing woman asked if I was lost and I told her no, I was just waiting for my session to start.

She said, "But you're blind!"

I put my cigarette out, and as I walked away, said to her, "Blind people break the law too, lady."

Honestly, I feel bad to this day about how I responded to her. On one hand, I was breaking a stereotype that she had in her mind of blind people, but I could have done it in a kinder way. That reminds me, don't put all blind people on a pedestal, we can be jerks too. We're all just human!

These days I'm helping people to disrupt their generalizations of others in a much gentler way. As my recovery progressed over the years, the chip on my shoulder was filled in and my attitude brightened. I've still got my sense of humor intact, and I'm seeing life through a different lens, you could say. Now, instead of lashing out as I did with that lady, I use my social media platforms to spread awareness and attempt to change how blind people are viewed. Anni and I create videos showing me doing anything from basic tasks like washing our car to more advanced things like changing the brake pads. There are times that people accuse me of faking my blindness because they are placing limits on what they believe blind people are capable of. Sometimes, I think people assume we are all just sitting at home on the couch doing nothing, when that couldn't be farther from the truth.

Anyway, as I said, making friends is often tough for blind people. So, I really valued my friendship with Chris and spent a lot of time at his house and woodshop. We would spend hours together, with Chris going through an encyclopedia of different types of wood, reading about them aloud to me and telling me their different colors and grain patterns.

Chris is low-vision, though, not totally blind like me. The vision that Chris has remaining allows him to still be able to read with a magnifier and navigate without a cane. He has one functioning eye at about 23/50 vision. Around ninety percent of blind people have some light perception and around ten percent are totally blind like me. Visual Impairment is an umbrella term and doesn't always mean totally blind; it's a spectrum. Each person has their own unique reason for their low vision or blindness. Sometimes it is from disease, genetics, and accidents, and sometimes people are born blind.

Blindness also looks different for each person. Some people have their eyes open, some closed, and some use sunglasses. Sunglasses can be used for light sensitivity or for privacy reasons, as some people want to cover their eyes. Some people see black or nothingness, and there are some, like me, who have very visual minds. Some experience haziness, blurry visuals, pinhole sight, and so on.

Chris and I shared a love for camping and target shooting. We found a beautiful place my uncle told me about in the mountains above Salt Lake City, where we lived. I was still living with my parents at this time. The camping spot was nice, because the road to it ended not far from where we were camping, and no one else really went there. It was almost as good as if we owned the place. It was a perfect spot for us to set up and shoot our black powder muzzleloaders at a hillside right across from the camp. We would just hang out and have a good time.

We had just your standard stuff the first year we were up there. We both had a sleeping bag and a tent. We also had some folding chairs with a nice folding table, along with some other gear, but not much else. Even though this was in the mountains, it got really hot there in the summertime. The first year we went, we spent all day chasing the shade around. About every twenty or thirty minutes, we'd have to drag our stuff to a new spot where the sun had shifted the shade. Though I couldn't see the sun, I sure felt it, and the shade was a nice break from the sweltering heat.

The second year we went up there, circa 2007, we brought a bit more stuff. We added canopies, cots, higher-quality sleeping bags, and cooking gear. My parents joked about how our campsite looked like a British officer's tent in a World War II movie, right down to the teapot.

The first year we went up there, we'd brought military MREs (Meals Ready-to-Eat) that we bought on the internet. It gave me a whole new respect for our soldiers because that stuff was not five-star cuisine by any means. And I know I'm kind of biased because, without a sense of smell, my sense of taste isn't as good as it could be. I was very ready to eat anything other than an MRE by the time we were done with that first camping trip. We would usually camp for between five to nine days. Over the years, we took four camping trips total to that spot.

Eventually, we started bringing a mix of MREs and tinfoil dinners. These were much more pleasant rations. One of the last times we went up, we made some practically gourmet dinners. We also brought ribs and chicken to cook in our Dutch oven. We even made a Dutch oven cake with some whipped cream for dessert. It was delicious!

Both Chris and I started forming a collection of muzzleloaders. The combination of scientific principles and rich historical background attracted me to black powder firearms. As a gift, I once gave Chris something called a cap-and-ball revolver, which is an old-fashioned black powder gun. I was spending a lot of time using his woodshop, and I wanted to show my gratitude.

Growing up, I went target shooting and hunting with my dad and brothers. It wasn't until several years after my attempt that I regained an interest in target shooting. It was something I deeply loved, and I'd been proud of my skills when I still had sight. Because I had adapted to so many other things, I decided I could probably pick up target shooting again. My

Working with Chris was always a rewarding experience, and my life wouldn't be the same without him. He taught me the skills that led me to my passion—and to the love of my life!

dad and I made one hell of a team. For the first couple of years, he would mostly stand behind me and give me directions. After I had started to gain ability in a different way, my dad tried different methods to help me reach the target. For instance, he would take an empty milk jug and throw it out in front of me so I could hear it roll. When it stopped, I would know where to shoot, which would make it roll again so I could track the sound. Another method he employed involved a rope and a bell.

Like camping and target shooting, Chris and I did a lot of things that folks might not expect blind people to be able to do. For instance, between February and June of 2009, I helped Chris build a 16' x 20' woodshop at his new house. But before we could get down to work on the shop, we first had to tackle a large patch of bamboo to make space to build. I owned a gardening machete, and it seemed like the perfect tool for the job. I crouched down so I could cut the stalks as low to the ground as possible and started hacking away. It was falling down over my back and piling up behind me as I cut. Chris steered clear by working across the yard where he was trimming an apple tree. I did a great job clearing the plant, but I wouldn't put my money on me leading a safari through the jungle anytime soon.

We started the shop by building a frame on the ground with 2' x 6' boards and covered that with plywood to make the floor. Since Chris already knew my level of experience, he had faith in me to assist with this job. We both used power drills and wood screws to put all the boards together. We built the walls on the floor and raised the frame to screw onto the base. We even installed the outlets and internal electric wiring for the shop, though my dad helped with running the power from the main breaker box out to the building. We were able to run a lathe, power saw, and air conditioner all at the same time. We managed to build a very nice wood shop, from the boards on the ground to the shingles on the roof, and everything in between.

The day we finished putting the insulation in the attic space, it was very hot, around 95 degrees Fahrenheit. As you can imagine, the attic was far hotter than that. It was the last day of construction, and we were putting up some wall panels, which are just heavy wafer boards. It didn't need to be anything fancy. The piece we were putting in was just a bit too long, and we were both getting tired. So instead of recutting it, I was using my body to smash it into place. I put my arms above my head and leaned my whole body into it, using as much force as I could when I hit the panels. Then, I felt a bit of a pop and a shift in my back. I thought, *Oh, that's going to hurt for a while.*

By no means did I think I had just crushed three vertebrae—the second time breaking my back. This was how I found out I have osteoporosis. I had no idea how badly I had injured myself because it did not hurt much. I was used to having chronic back pain because of messing up my back years before that.

I went home after finishing the woodshop and went to sleep. At 3 a.m., I woke up with excruciating pain in my back and my left shoulder. I went to the doctor the next day, and I was not taken very seriously at first, with no X-rays being done.

I went on with life, and about four days later, I went camping with Chris for nine days up in the wilderness. When we returned, it felt like I had a golf ball under the skin of my back because the swelling had become so bad. I went back to the same doctor, and this time they x-rayed me and saw that I had crushed the three vertebrae: T6, T8, and T9. One was fifty-five percent crushed and called a "burst" because the fracture went completely through it, front to back, top to bottom, and broke one of the little joints off the side. They sent me to an orthopedic doctor to help with my recovery. This doctor performed a bone density scan and found that I had osteoporosis, which I was told is very uncommon in young men.

That summer, I had to wear a back brace that felt and looked like body armor. It consisted of one hard plastic plate that covered most of my chest and another one that covered most of my back. It had a bar that came up in front, with two pads to ensure that I stayed upright. It was fully wrapped in Velcro, which made it feel like a heavy sweater-vest. Salt Lake City in the summertime gets pretty hot, so outdoor temperatures were between the upper 90s and lower 100s, I was rather uncomfortable!

In addition to the physical therapy my doctor prescribed, I added some self-imposed physical therapy, which was woodworking. I was lucky all I needed was physical therapy and no surgery.

I was healing from this injury for about two months. During that time, I made a very intricate table that I am extremely proud of. I like to call it the crown jewel of my woodworking career. The table is made of Padauk and yellowheart woods. It took me about 400 hours to make. It's made of forty-six separate pieces of wood, and because the lathe is my favorite tool, I incorporated as much turning as I could. The contrasting color design of the table was partially inspired by lamps I had already built. The table has two drawers, one on top and one on the bottom. On the very top, there is a beautiful knot, which people have told me resembles an eye or a hurricane. The table would play a huge role in my life. First, it helped me recover from my broken back. Later, and arguably more importantly, it would play a vital role in my future, even leading me to meet my wife.

At one point, Chris told me about a school in Washington State that taught piano tuning and repair to blind people. His father-in-law, who was a piano tuner, went to the school in the 1960s. It had been several years since I had stopped working with vocational rehab, and I was getting antsy trying to figure out what I would do for employment and get my life going.

When he told me about the school, it sounded perfect to me. I looked it up and called them. They invited me to come do a three-day trial to ensure I had the proper mechanical aptitude to learn how to work on pianos.

In 2009, I flew to Washington state for my trial at the school. It immediately felt like the place that I had been waiting to find my whole life. Though I was blind to the state's beautiful surroundings, I could feel the presence of the tall trees, and the air felt invigorating. I felt deep down inside me that this was where I was supposed to be.

I had my first trial day at the piano school in October of 2009. I felt welcomed and included from the moment I arrived. I couldn't wait to get the rest of my life started. The program seemed really fun, and I was sure it would hold my interest. I was eager to learn all I could. I had no idea what an incredible piece of equipment a piano is. For the first three days, they had me tune a note or two on the piano, feel around the mechanical parts, and manipulate them a bit to see if I had the dexterity required for the work. They decided I had the right stuff, so I started working with vocational rehab again to get the funding I needed to attend the school. There were a lot of details to work out, such as where I would live. Despite having a lot to figure out, it felt so good to finally have a new direction in my life. The school did not have an opening for me right away, so in the meantime, I prepared myself to make the move by saving money, and I was still woodworking with Chris.

In November of 2009, that same year, my back was finally all healed up and I had an upcoming appointment to see my doctor for one last checkup. I went to sleep one night, and when I woke up, I was on a stretcher in a vehicle driving down the road. Someone was sitting next to me, and I asked them where we were going. The person was a paramedic, and they told me that I'd had a seizure, and we were on our way to the hospital.

I thought, *Okay, well, I guess this is new.*

Building this table was one of the most pivotal moments of my life, though I didn't know it yet. In many ways, I owe it all to this table.

I didn't quite know what to think, but I had no intention of delaying my plans to move to Washington. It would have taken losing a foot or something extreme to stop me from going. Even then, just give me a box to stand on and I'll get it done. I wasn't about to let another setback get in the way of my dreams.

At that point, I had been accepted to the piano repair school and would be going there in February of 2011, which was a little over one year away. This seizure was how I found out I have post-traumatic epilepsy from my suicide attempt. One of the very deceptive things about post-traumatic epilepsy is a time period called the honeymoon phase. It can be inactive for long periods of time after a traumatic brain injury. The time between the injury and the onset of epilepsy can last months to years. In my case, it was twelve years between the attempt and when I had my first seizure.

The seizure was so intense that it caused me to break my back again. I re-broke T6 and newly broke T7. The back brace had to go back on for a few months. The only time I could take it off was when I showered. I had to sleep with that brace on, as well. If I even stretched the wrong way, I could do major damage to my spine. The second time around, it was nice to have that brace, because Salt Lake City gets pretty cold in winter. This time, I didn't mind the extra layer of insulation. I guess you have to find the silver lining wherever you can!

Though that year was full of more struggles, I could feel the excitement building in me about moving onward to my new life. I never really felt any fear about starting the piano rebuilding program, but I did feel a little impatient. I felt like this was the adventure I had been preparing for, and it seemed like something I could do and use to make a living.

I continued physical therapy and kept living life relatively normally. I took the bus to Chris's house to continue working on the table, my masterpiece. I'm sure the woodworking I was still doing helped a lot in my back recovery.

I could have viewed these setbacks as signs that I wasn't meant to go, but I felt in my heart I needed to persevere once again.

I was doing lots of lathe work, which involved standing and using my arms to hold the chisel in place up to the spinning piece of wood. After I assembled the table, I had to sand. And sand. And sand. I sanded that table for weeks. When I put the drawer boxes on the table, the seams weren't quite perfect, so I had to use a power sander to get all the joints just right. Unfortunately, I messed up some of the rings on the posts, but I was able to fix them by hand. When it comes to my woodworking, I am a bit of a perfectionist. I take pride in the work that I do, so I'm very picky about my craftsmanship.

It was woodworking that brought me to piano work, and it was piano work that brought me to my new life, and eventually, my love. Sometimes detours can be opportunities. I could have viewed these setbacks as signs that I wasn't meant to go, but I felt in my heart I needed to persevere once again. Keep on truckin', as they say!

CHAPTER 4

Rebirth

— JOHN —

I like to call the first year and a half in Washington my "college years." At this point, I was still using substances to cope, but meth was off the table for good. It had almost killed me, and I wasn't going to let it get in the way of the life I envisioned for myself. Tackling addiction is a lifelong undertaking. It doesn't happen overnight, and the struggles that come with it never fully disappear.

I was still drinking heavily, chasing the feeling of numbness and the temporary peace it brought. Even though my life was taking an upward turn, the demons I had wrestled with my whole life—anxiety, depression, and isolation—were still with me. A lot of those feelings were of loneliness and longing for a life companion.

Initially, when I moved to Washington state, I was placed in a small house next to the piano repair school. It was a house set up for two people, so I had a roommate. It was convenient that it was directly next to the school. The commute was about a hundred feet, if that.

Working on a piano is mainly fine-tuned woodworking. Most of the instruments are made of wood, leather, or felt. When I'd been working on that padauk and yellowheart table, I often wished I could turn my woodworking hobby into a living. The piano work felt pretty close to woodworking, and it kept my hands and mind busy.

The school had a schedule with classes, just like any learning institution. In the mornings, our head teacher would go over terminology. Then, he would assign daily tasks such as tuning, learning how to regulate (calibrate) a piano, and various minor repairs and replacement processes. The majority of my first semester was taken up by learning to tune. Tuning a piano is a complex process, and it took me a long time to learn. It was frustrating, and I didn't care for it. I would obsess about getting each note just right,

I believe blindness has brought out the bravery in me. I have done things as a blind person that took lots of courage.

The only adaptive tool in my workshop is the Rotomatic, which I use to measure.

and it would sometimes take me days to tune one piano. I'd always been a perfectionist. In many ways, this has helped me in my life. In other ways, it's caused me to heap a lot of unneeded pressure on myself and fueled my anxiety. I'm sure this was part of my struggle with tuning pianos, but ultimately, it just wasn't my cup of tea.

I *did* love all the mechanics involved in piano work. The number of parts astonished me. Each piano had 11,000 separate parts on average. Some had more than 12,000, depending on the size of the instrument! Making all these distinct parts work together in unison required care and precision, and I found the work rewarding.

As I got more involved in the repair work, I knew I would need a measuring device to work on pianos. As mentioned, I had previously been using a Click Rule with woodworking, but I discovered another device that worked better for me: the Rotomatic. The Rotomatic is essentially a finely machined bolt that is flattened on both sides, other than a tab every one-half inch along one side. It has a large, rectangular-shaped nut, each full turn of which indicates one-sixteenth of an inch. It has extensions measuring six inches, twelve inches, and eighteen inches. It's much smaller than a Click Rule, which made it easier to navigate the smaller spaces of a piano. While I originally started using this for the piano work, I still use it today in my woodworking. I'm able to work more quickly with the Rotomatic, as I find it's more accurate and the ease of turning the nut to measure works better for me.

Six months after starting at the piano hospital, I moved into a small apartment complex near the school. My criminal record made it challenging to find housing, but the place I found was a good fit. No longer having a roommate, this was another significant step toward me feeling more independent.

I made friends with some people there right away, and since we were all relatively young men who were still single, it could get a little rowdy. The apartment complex was basically like a frat house. After my school day and on weekends, we would spend time drinking, listening to music, and grilling food. That feeling of loneliness I had felt most of my life subsided. My new friends didn't treat me differently because of my blindness, and I felt like I belonged.

I was attending school full-time, and things were going really well. I was progressing with my program, at least in terms of the mechanical work, but tuning pianos was still my biggest barrier. Early on in my program, I met Rick Patten. Rick had been a piano rebuilder for many years and was one of the best in the business. He had a shop near the school that was full of supplies and materials, and he would often partner with the school on jobs. He did all their major rebuilds. We got to know each other through the school, and one day I showed him the table I had built. He was impressed with my work, seeing potential in me, and believed I would be able to learn advanced piano repair methods. This small moment would prove life-changing, as this was how the table I took such pride in would eventually lead me to meet my wife, Anni. If it weren't for this impromptu exchange, Rick might not have taken me on as his apprentice, and it was my work with Rick outside of the school that resulted in that fateful meeting.

Rick and I became good friends immediately. My other closest friends at this time were Joe and TJ. They lived in the same apartment complex as me. The best way to describe Joe is crusty on the outside, with a heart of gold on the inside. He was a twenty-year army veteran who had been a drill sergeant and combat engineer. Joe and I got along very well. We identified with each other in many ways. Just like most of my close relationships, Joe was about twenty years older than me, but we shared many good times together. Sadly, Joe passed away in February of 2023.

TJ was one of the nicest people I've ever known. We shared a close bond, and he had an intuitive ability to know exactly how to help me. I'll never forget the time we went miniature golfing, as it was an amazing experience, and much of that is owed to TJ's friendship and thoughtfulness. I was able to get par on almost every hole. When we got to each new hole, TJ would take his clubs and tap on the places that I needed to avoid so I would know how to hit my golf ball. It worked out well.

Something I felt that I had robbed myself of in my early twenties was my independence. I wished I had the freedom to explore and hop in my car on my own whenever I wanted. These feelings of regret were probably what fueled a lot of my drug use during my years as a young man. On the other hand, I believe blindness has brought out the bravery in me. I have done things as a blind person that took lots of courage.

This new time in Washington felt like a do-over, a chance to live independently and successfully. I was living on my own and cooking for myself. I upgraded from hard-boiled eggs to frozen dinners, and occasionally TJ and I cooked together. Most of what I was eating was just stuff I threw in the microwave, but this was accessible for me. It was a far cry from the cups of noodles I had somehow lived on in Craig. Once, a friend took me grocery shopping, and along with my usual supply of microwave meals, I got some apples and oranges. My friend jokingly asked me if I thought my system could handle the shock that would come with eating such healthy food. My life had improved considerably, and I felt invested in it and myself.

As I mentioned, this do-over I'd been afforded provided me lots of opportunities to do new, sometimes scary, things. Each new experience brought with it another degree of independence, but I also found myself learning when to lean on others for support. A good example of that is another time I went grocery shopping, this time on my own. I took the bus from my new apartment to the store. As I left the store, I had one big, heavy bag of groceries in one hand, and my cane in the other. The weight of the bag made me list to one side like a poorly balanced ship. I drifted to that side as I was walking, causing me to make two giant circles in the parking lot before I found my way back to the store. I decided to throw in the towel and call for a ride.

It wasn't all roses during this time, of course. I struggled very much with alcoholism, and it got worse and worse until I met Anni. It continued for a while after that, as well. Before I met Anni, I had been alone for a long time. This was hard for me. I wanted to find a companion to spend my life with. I was happy to have my friendships, but there were many lonely days. Meeting people is so challenging as a blind person. So much of human interaction is visual, and people don't often think about how that aspect can shape our experiences and relationships. Anyone who struggles with feelings of isolation can tell you how they can stand in a crowd of 10,000 people and still feel alone. But, for a blind person, this feeling is compounded by the fact that we are cut off from all visual cues, truly alone in that darkness.

Anyone who struggles with feelings of isolation can tell you how they can stand in a crowd of 10,000 people and still feel alone. But, for a blind person, this feeling is compounded by the fact that we are cut off from all visual cues, truly alone in that darkness.

I didn't even know how to meet someone or talk to them, so I just existed.

As I forged more friendships and other friendships deepened, I started some new hobbies, as well. One of those was gardening. Our town's local community center had a large plot of land, and people could rent individual lots. The spaces were 20' x 20' and could be used for people to grow their own gardens. TJ decided to get two plots, and he asked me if I wanted to join him. I said yes right away. The community center was within easy walking distance of our apartment complex, so it was nice to take a walk every few days to water and weed the garden. This was in the spring of 2012, and while I enjoyed these little moments at the time, it turned out that the garden would play a huge role in my life. Little did I know that I would be getting married to the love of my life three years later in front of that very same garden patch.

I love peas, so one of the first things I did was to plant a huge pea patch. It's common to use trellises to grow them. Instead, I weaved twine about a foot off the ground, with some stakes going around the perimeter of the patch and the twine weaving back and forth between the stakes. I used old piano keys for the stakes. It looked similar to a giant spiderweb. My pea patch turned into a big, tangled hedge of peas, and my crop was bountiful.

When I started planting the peas, TJ was planting a large crop of corn. He looked over at me. I was down on my knees digging through the dirt with my hands, breaking it up to get it ready to plant the peas. He said, with some surprise in his voice, "Oh, I see you meant you really want to garden!"

I laughed and said, "What else did you think I was going to do?"

I stepped into my workroom, and I met the love of my life, Anni, my future wife, who is a gifted artist.

Even so, I knew what he meant. A lot of times, people will say that they want to do something, and they end up just watching the other person. I had no intention of doing that. I wanted to be involved and loved getting my hands dirty. I was grateful for TJ's patience and gardening expertise. I learned a lot from him during this time.

Around then, I'd been learning the more advanced rebuild techniques for pianos. I was working very closely with Rick on many extra projects so I could learn everything I could. One of the things that we worked together on was a complex set of jigs to allow blind people to replace grand piano hammers easily. Rick had the mind of an engineer, blended with that of an artist and a designer. He'd developed this jig system over a few years and was basically done with it, and I was helping him find the places that needed to be improved. Because Rick is not blind, there were some things that he did not think of as a sighted person. I showed him the little pieces that needed to be changed, and we made a great team. This mentorship and extra work would prove pivotal in many ways.

In July of 2012, I had another life-changing experience. I'd started my final project that summer, which was restringing and replacing hammers in a piano. The school was closed and wasn't offering classes during this

On the day we met, Anni was working with a group of kids from a local homeless shelter to paint a piano at the piano-repair school where I worked and studied. The theme the kids had chosen was "love."

time, but it was still open as a business. I was working closely with Rick, who was a mentor to me at this point. He was supervising a piano rebuild for the school, which I was assisting with.

I needed to get some work done one afternoon, so I headed into the school. I stepped into my workroom, and I met the love of my life, Anni, my future wife, who is a gifted artist.

She was volunteering for a fundraiser that the school did every year. They asked local artists to volunteer to paint a piano, which would then be placed in the community and sponsored by a business for people to play and enjoy.

The first thing I did when I walked into the room was put my hand in wet paint on a piano. Remembering that there would be artists for the fundraiser at the school that day, I thought to myself, *Oh great. I just poked out Mona Lisa's eyes*, thinking I might've ruined someone's painting.

Luckily, the artist was just priming it, and she told me a group of kids she was working with would be adding the details on the piano. We both laughed and introduced ourselves. I think my face might've turned a bit red. I thought she had a nice, melodious voice and a calm, warm presence.

We had a nice conversation, just kind of chitchat. We talked about where I came from and Vancouver, Washington, where she was born and raised. I found out she had been an artist for most of her life, had done gallery shows all over the area, and sold her art. She was heavily involved in the community and told me she organized events such as fundraisers, art shows, and even a music festival.

One of the first things she said to me was that she loved my hands, and I taught her a little bit about how pianos worked. We listened to music that played from my phone as we each worked on our projects, me across the room from her. There were things about that day that did not feel like a coincidence, things that felt like this meeting was in the stars, as they say. I would later find out that the theme of the piano was "love," a theme chosen by the kids Anni was working with on the project. I was working on things called bridle straps. Could this be a foreshadowing of our life together? Maybe, if you believe in that sort of thing. And I do.

Over the next week or so, I started the first major rebuild project that I ever did. I replaced the strings and hammers on a five-foot Cable-Nelson grand piano, a 1920s vintage. Anni was painting her themed piano at that same time. We ran into each other a few more times in the school. I was happy to bump into her, and I loved when she was around. But since I had the bravery of George McFly from *Back to the Future* when it came to talking to women, I never asked Anni if she wanted to go out. I got lucky, though. She called me one day out of the blue and asked me if I wanted to go on a date with her.

When she called, I was sitting at my apartment, hanging out with Rick and TJ. She asked if I wanted to go out, and I froze because I was broke. After a pause, I said I would call her back. I racked my brain trying to think of a no-cost date idea that wouldn't make me seem like a cheapskate. Rick and TJ were happy for me because they knew that I had been lonely and wanted to find some companionship.

I remembered I had a lot of peas that needed to be harvested. I knew she was into nature, so I thought she might like to see my garden. I told my friends about my idea of picking peas, and they started teasing me about it, which was funny, but I was still nervous.

It could backfire on me like one of those dating shows when they ask the two people separate from each other how the date went. The guy says, "I think it went great. We went to my garden and picked peas. It was nice." And then they interview the woman, and she says, "He *made* me pick peas. I can hardly believe it! I am not his gardener."

But I was willing to risk it, and I'm glad I did.

From what I had learned of Anni so far, I believed she would love that kind of thing, so I called her back and asked if she would like to come to my garden and help me pick peas. She said yes right away, and I could hear the excitement in her voice. I could tell that she liked the idea. Phew!

I was nervous, but happy that maybe I had finally met someone. Still, I didn't want to get my hopes too high. We enjoyed many of the same things, and I felt safe around her. I was also happy that she liked my pea-picking idea, because it meant she was down-to-earth.

On the date, I realized that I might have found my person, and I fell in love a little bit that very night. We talked for a few hours, picking peas in the tangled hedge that was my garden. I was happier than I had been in a long time.

CHAPTER 5

Love Is Blind

ANNI

Our second date came about a week after our first date in the pea patch. We were both busy people, John with his apprenticeship at the piano repair school and me with a job in the library and my volunteer work. During that time, I was in what would prove to be my last year at the library. I had been working there for more than fourteen years, doing everything from shelving books, answering information requests that came in by telephone, school visits, after-school programs, and story times. It was a fulfilling job, but art was calling to me, and it was time for me to pursue that aspect of myself again. I wouldn't actually work as a full-time artist until 2019, but that part of my story will come later!

For our second date, I was going to bring some takeout to his apartment, and we were going to "watch" a movie together. I would learn quickly that even though John was blind, it was common for him to use terms like watch, see, and look. They were all just figures of speech to him—we just saw things differently.

I was again feeling really nervous. We hadn't talked much over the phone that week, and it felt like a thousand years had passed since our first date. I picked up tacos from my favorite local restaurant and headed over to his place.

This time when he answered the door, the light was on in his living room. He had the same wide grin on his face that I remembered. His dimples created divots in each cheek, and his cleft chin was visible through a small patch of a goatee. I wondered to myself if he shaved his own face and then remembered he told me he cut his own hair, which was a dark, short crew cut.

John is extraordinary not just because of his blindness, but because of his attitude in life. He does things his own way, not caring about society's standards or expectations.

He turned and stepped back, gesturing with his arm for me to come inside. He had a proud look on his face and said, "I remembered to turn the light on for you."

It occurred to me how incredibly thoughtful that was. He showed me again and again how big his heart was. We sat down in some pink, velvet swivel chairs that had been gifted to him from a local church. I realized that the color probably didn't matter to a man who couldn't see.

Because he didn't have a television, he suggested we watch something on his smartphone. He opened Netflix and we watched a show that would become a favorite over the years: *Bob's Burgers*. I wasn't a fancy lady, so this was the perfect kind of date for me. Low-pressure, quiet, and intimate.

While we ate our tacos, we chatted about our lives. I told him about my two sisters, one four years older than me at the time who had three boys (my niece would be born a few years later). I also had a sister twelve years younger than me (who had her first baby, my nephew, in November of 2023). My parents were still together, and my family was close.

John told me that his folks were still together, as well, and he had five siblings—two sisters and three brothers. John was the baby. He had lost count of how many nieces and nephews he had, but he thought it was around twenty-six (the total has now moved up to thirty-eight nieces and nephews between our two families). I raised my eyebrows and then he made a wholesome joke about his family being Mormon. I giggled and told him I came from a Catholic upbringing and large families were also common in my family's church.

As we talked about our families, the conversation turned to our childhoods. It sounded like we had a similar upbringing, as we were both raised in religious households but were no longer part of the churches we were raised in. Our families loved and accepted us, just as we loved and accepted them. It was nice to hear, and it didn't surprise me he came from a loving family.

I finally got up the courage to ask him how he became blind. He took a deep breath. I momentarily regretted asking him until he reassured me it was okay that I asked.

I did not expect what he said next.

"I am a suicide survivor."

My eyes filled with tears as he told me that he had attempted suicide at age sixteen by shooting himself. He didn't go into too much detail, but this further explained the nerve damage that I learned about on our first date. The nerve damage he endured was so extreme that he didn't have control over opening and closing his eyes. His optic nerves and his sinus pathways had been destroyed, as well. He was left completely blind, and unlike some people with diminished vision, he had absolutely no light perception.

I really didn't know how to respond. He could tell I was getting emotional and apologized for upsetting me.

That night, we bonded over our traumas and our triumphs. We had both faced the darkness and come out the other side.

"You have nothing to apologize for," I said. "Thank you so much for telling me that. I can't imagine how hard that must have been for you."

I then told him of my own history with depression and eating disorders. I, too, had attempted suicide at a young age but was lucky it hadn't resulted in any permanent damage.

That night, we bonded over our traumas and our triumphs. We had both faced the darkness and come out the other side. I saw a lot of myself in John. We shared similar mental health struggles, and I, too, had felt like an outcast most of my life, and had overcome many daunting obstacles from my childhood. As an adult, I struggled with alcohol dependency, though I quit drinking by my early 30s. I think John was surprised when I told him of my past, maybe a little taken aback that we were able to be so open and vulnerable with each other so quickly.

At one point, I looked over and he had a soft smile on his face. He stood up and slowly navigated over to my chair. He held out his hand and I took it. He set his other hand on top of mine, sandwiching it gingerly.

He knelt in front of where I was sitting and asked, "Would it be okay if I felt what you look like?"

My face flushing, I told him that would be lovely.

Reaching up to my face, he softly felt my cheeks and my forehead, and when he got to my glasses, I removed them so he could feel my eyes.

He leaned in closer to me, and I realized he was coming in for a kiss, and I leaned into it.

We kissed softly. Then, leaning back, I laughed and asked, "Do you regularly feel what people look like, or was that a way to get close to me?"

John chuckled, shrugged, and said, "A blind guy only has so many moves."

Later that night, I wrote in my journal that this felt like the beginning of a beautiful love story. And I was right.

Our courtship continued, though to be quite honest, it could be awkward at times for many reasons. John had been sowing his wild oats, so to speak, living on his own successfully for the first time in his life. We had both been single for more than five years, so adapting to a new person in our lives meant changing some things. When I met John, neither of us was expecting to face such significant challenges. We had both been living lives of solitude and were used to our own ways of living.

We both felt ready for a serious commitment, but the logistics of how to make that work was a horse of a different color, as they say. And dating someone with a visual impairment was new territory for me. I didn't want to say or do the wrong thing.

In the beginning, I was careful not to say "blind," but quickly learned it wasn't a bad word. Nor is the word "disabled" disfavored, at least not by John. I was skirting my way around the words by saying "visual impairment," "differently abled," etc., but John told me he preferred to use "blind" and "disabled." I now understand that, while the replacement terms are preferred by some people, this can vary greatly. I was grateful for the lessons but still felt like I was tiptoeing around things for a while until I got it right. John was a patient teacher, however. He was quick to answer any questions, and due to my naturally curious nature, I had many!

I kept feeling the need to do things for him, simple tasks like opening doors or speaking for him when we were out in public. I did everything wrong that I could get wrong, and soon realized that trial and error might be the only way I was going to discover the right ways to address these matters. I learned to ask before I did anything related to helping him, and thus came to understand that I should not doubt him and his abilities.

I had to overcome a lot of my own biases regarding blindness. One of the best ways to do this was to admit that I had them. I assumed blindness meant complete reliance on others. I was so wrong!

I eventually got into the groove with John. He would open doors for me and even bring me flowers that he picked from his apartment complex. We talked about our past relationships and the lessons we learned from them. There were mistakes we didn't want to repeat, patterns that we wanted to break. I think part of our success was facing these difficult conversations head-on early in our romance. Neither one of us has ever shied away from solving our problems together, though it took some practice in the beginning.

He was still holding onto the party phase of his life by a thread, and that was often a source of contention between us. I had quit drinking alcohol for the most part, and I had totally quit smoking cigarettes the year before. I didn't really have any issues with other people drinking, but at the time, he was drinking heavily and smoking a pack a day. I tried giving him his freedom to live his life as he wanted, but it did affect me. If it weren't for the fact that John and I had a soulful connection, those things would have been deal-breakers for me. We would later face these issues again and again, more often successfully than not.

On one of our dates, I asked John if he'd like to spend the night at my house. I was living with roommates at the time, good friends that felt like family. I was looking forward to introducing them to John.

First, we went out to dinner at a local steakhouse. It was our first date out in public, and I found myself curious about the way John navigated his plate of food. He used his fingers to feel around, and I pointed out where certain items were in front of him.

When the check arrived, I quickly realized I hadn't thought of how we would handle this and asked how he wanted to proceed. He had earlier told me he wanted the meal to be his treat, so he asked if I would read the total of the bill to him. He paid with a debit card. I helped fill in the tip on the receipt and directed his finger to the signature line. I was surprised by how legible his signature was. Later, I learned that when he paid with cash for items, he kept his bills folded in different patterns. One-dollar bills were left unfolded, fives were in half lengthwise, tens were halved widthwise once, and twenties were folded twice widthwise. His wallet had two different bill compartments, and he used these to separate large and small denominations.

Learning little details like this became the norm and were great lessons in going with the flow. John is extraordinary not just because of his blindness, but because of his attitude in life. He does things his own way, not caring about society's standards or expectations.

I would learn quickly that he was a people-pleaser like me, and we both struggled with feelings that we sometimes disappointed others. We each had an innate inclination toward perfectionism, which branched out into most areas of our lives. This included how we were perceived by others. Never wanting to appear disrespectful or confrontational, being agreeable was often the easier option. This came in handy in our relationship, as it made us considerate. But, over the years, in our own ways, we've found our own voices. Authenticity has become an important value for both of us, meaning we can now say how we really feel, respectfully. The confidence we've gained from this has led us to learn how to be more assertive and resolute.

When I asked John if he'd like to stay over, he readily accepted. That night was the first night John slept at my place. Intimacy between us had already made us comfortable with each other, but sleeping in the same bed was new territory. My double bed was more comfortable for one, and because we had been single for so long, we valued our independence. I did love the thought of falling asleep in his arms, though.

Later that night, I awoke with a start. I heard quick breathing like someone hyperventilating. I threw on the lights and there was John next to me, having a grand mal seizure. He hadn't told me yet that he had epilepsy, and I had never seen anyone have such an episode.

I quickly turned him on his side and called out for my roommate. I can't remember fully, but I think I was the one who called 911, and my roommate reassured me he was going to be okay. Her calming presence helped me and soothed my anxiety.

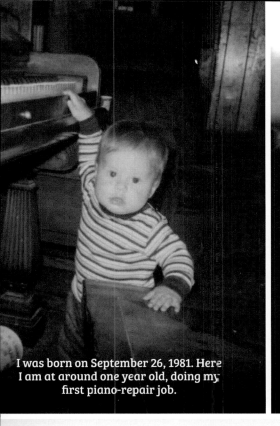

I was born on September 26, 1981. Here I am at around one year old, doing my first piano-repair job.

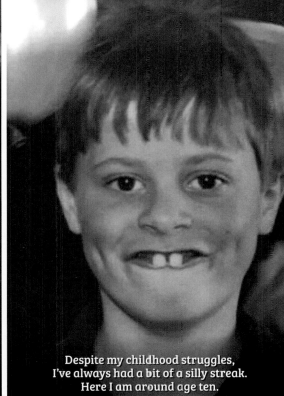

Despite my childhood struggles, I've always had a bit of a silly streak. Here I am around age ten.

I come from a large family. I have three brothers and two sisters. I am the baby of the bunch. Pictured here is Kristi, Bill, Rick, Mike, Kellie, Mom (Karen), me, and Dad (Alan).

I lost my sight on April 10th, 1998 at the age of sixteen. Though I outwardly appeared to be a happy-go-lucky kid, I wrestled with depression, anxiety, and feelings of isolation.

I broke my back for the second time in June of 2009, and had to wear a back brace in the sweltering heat. It didn't slow me down for long, though!

I took my first woodworking class in late 2005. My teacher, Chris Hathaway, quickly became my mentor, and I worked with him at his home woodshop from 2006–2011.

Here I am in 2017, revisiting the wall that caused me to break my back when I helped Chris build a woodshop in 2009.

Chris and I remained steadfast friends
over the years.

Chris and I took this photo in front of the shop
we built when I took a trip back to Utah in 2017.

The piano Anni was painting just before we met.

The children from the shelter working
on their designs for the piano decorations.

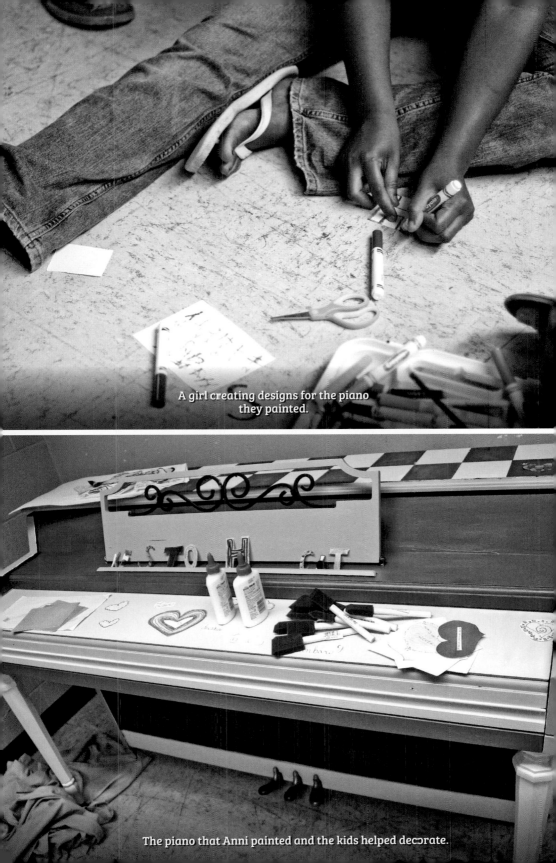

A girl creating designs for the piano they painted.

The piano that Anni painted and the kids helped decorate.

Anni snapped this photo of me while I was working on some piano repairs in the same classroom. I'd been making pieces called bridle straps.

Anni took this picture of me and my winning smile while I worked in the classroom we shared that day.

I'm pictured here building centerpiece planters for a fundraiser at Evergreen Habitat for Humanity in 2016, Vancouver, WA.

We had our first date in July of 2012, shortly after meeting at the "Piano Hospital." We picked peas in my community garden plot.

On that first date, Anni snapped a photo of my Eye of Horus tattoo. The tattoo serves as a reminder of how important my hands are to me, as they are how I "see" the world.

We were married on September 12th, 2015. We had the ceremony in the garden plot where we had our first date. We spent several months tending the garden before the big day.

Our first dance.
Photo taken by Niki Haney.

As a symbol of our love and dedication to grow together, we watered our garden together in front of our assembled friends and family. Photo taken by Niki Haney.

We were delighted to share our cherished day with so many friends
and family. Here, I'm posing with my proud mom and dad.
Photo by Niki Haney.

Anni and I strive to find joy in all life's little moments together—such as playing in the snow!

WASHOUGAL STUDIO ARTISTS TOUR

We started working as full-time artists in 2019. Here we are readying for a studio tour. Guests would come through the house to watch Anni create, then head to my woodshop out back to watch me work.

Us on the steps of our home shortly after moving in together.

We've shared countless adventures and weathered many hardships over the years. Through it all, we have supported and encouraged each other without fail.

Our little family.

I took this picture of Anni during our trip
to the Olympic Peninsula.

Here I am standing on a dock at the
Columbia River, circa 2018.

I had a lot of fun flying a kite by the ocean in Long Beach, WA, 2017.

Me by the Columbia River, circa 2018.

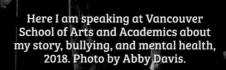

Here I am speaking at Vancouver School of Arts and Academics about my story, bullying, and mental health, 2018. Photo by Abby Davis.

Me and "The Blood Bowl."

Here I am working as a volunteer to help paint a house with Habitat for Humanity, circa 2016.

I became Anni's favorite subject to photograph. Here's a picture she took of me on the beach, circa 2018.

Here, Pickle and I contemplate a swim.

I've always loved animals, and really enjoyed feeding this baby goat!

A handful of shavings from my turnings.

I sat with John as he started breathing normally again, the blue pallor on his face reverting to its normal color. After a seizure, a person can be very disoriented, and it can take some time for their memory and comprehension to return to normal. It is essentially like sleepwalking.

I could tell that John's episode was ending. Suddenly, he stood up on the bed, and before I could stop him, he started walking across it. He stepped onto a cedar chest placed at the end of the bed that had a large, concrete Buddha statue on it. He badly scraped his shin on the statue, and it started to bleed. Later, he would tell me that he'd been disoriented and thought he was at his own house.

I helped him back to the bed, and as he lay there, I told him the paramedics were on the way. I asked him if he was okay. He nodded and turned his head toward me. He held my hand and said, "I love you."

It was the first time he said it to me, and later I would tease him, asking if it still counted even though he couldn't remember what year it was at the time. He reassured me that it counted!

The paramedics arrived and asked John questions like what year it was, who was the president, and how old he was. He got them all wrong. He was about four years off on every answer. They told me not to worry, as this was common after a seizure, and he would regain his memory later.

John would have other seizures over the next couple years, and they were always terrifying to witness. With the correct medication, and since he's mostly quit drinking (except for the occasional holiday whiskey), he no longer has these scary episodes.

I followed the ambulance to the hospital and arrived at John's room where a doctor was examining him.

During the examination, he lifted John's eyelids one at a time, and for the first time, I was able to see his eyes. They were not what I expected. They were a light bluish white, lightly covered in scar tissue. I gasped. They were beautiful.

About a week earlier, I had a vivid dream that John opened his eyes. In the dream, his eyes were filled with a nebula. Being an artist, I sketched a cosmic, nebula-filled eye. It wasn't the last time John inspired me creatively.

As our romance continued, I think a lot of people around us saw a fairy tale, but the first six months were nothing but trial and struggle. We fought almost every day, and I didn't know if we were going to make it. Our disagreements generally started because of John's drinking. He would sometimes nod off when we were hanging out. At first, I thought it was due to his blindness and insomnia, but eventually realized he was drinking excessively. Our relationship greatly improved once he stopped drinking about a year and a half after we met.

John was fiercely independent, which I loved. I was also very independent and loved the freedom that my artistic lifestyle gave to me. We each struggled with integrating our lifestyles together, and this sometimes brought conflict into our relationship. John didn't like having "checks and balances" on his life, so to speak. I understood this, but I also knew if we wanted to grow as a couple, we'd have to start making compromises.

I was grateful that John had his own life, his own friends, and his own interests. Our independence meant that our courtship moved a little slower than most. I think this was to our benefit in the end.

John lived with his parents for many years in Salt Lake before moving to Vancouver. He was finally living successfully on his own, and I didn't want to intrude on his newfound autonomy.

On the other side of things, I was used to going to events out in the community regularly. I went to art walks, concerts, fundraisers, business openings—all things that John didn't find blind-friendly. Meeting new people was difficult for him, and it overwhelmed him to be surrounded by crowds with a lot of noise. Sighted people can sometimes feel awkward approaching a blind person, which left John feeling a bit lonely out in public. We started going to some events together, and I reminded my friends to please introduce themselves by name when talking to him. He said that voices mostly sound generic to him, and remembering names was also difficult because he couldn't put a face to them. I learned to give him little anecdotes about each person he was introduced to. "Sarah the musician, Leah the wine bar owner, Dan the theater owner, Christopher the poet," were some helpful ways to keep John included.

I wanted so desperately for us to work out, but each day brought on a new challenge for us. Something I did know about each of us was that we had both faced huge challenges and come out stronger on the other side. This felt no different.

We discovered a way to create a connection through what we called "blind experiments." With a blindfold on, I would take on simple tasks that John deals with on a daily basis. These types of experiments are controversial in some circles because they can create a false picture of blindness. It's not exactly an accurate representation, since most people with blindness have gone through some sort of mobility training or have been without sight long enough to adapt. This was a loose version of blindness, but we found benefit from them anyway.

The first blind experiment we did was counting change. Before we started, I remember thinking how easy it was going to be. I assumed that feeling the sizes of each coin would be simple. I was very wrong! Not only was I dealing with the sudden darkness of the room, I started doubting myself in different ways. The first emotion I remember feeling was that of being scared.

My impulse was to pull the blindfold up and peek, but I fought it. John didn't have a choice; he was permanently blind. I wanted to feel that permanency somehow, even though it was actually temporary for me.

I got braver with each experiment. One time, he led me out to the street (luckily, I lived on a very slow road), and I was forced to trust him, and myself, completely.

It felt like we were slowly building a layer of faith with each trial we accomplished together. I felt us growing and blossoming together. Temporarily losing my sight was jarring. There was a whirlwind of feelings: fear, anxiety, exhilaration, and frustration.

It helped that John was so patient with me. He told me he had to learn patience after becoming blind. Every step he took was a potential danger. Every time he dropped something and bent over to pick it up, there was the possibility of hitting his head on a nearby table or shelf. In addition to the tools he'd learned in his mobility and orientation training, slowing down was the only way he'd get through life and do it without harming himself.

I have always struggled with impatience, but being with John has been the biggest lesson of my life. Because of his focus on the present moment, he enjoys life on a different level than I'm used to. I had been doing yoga and meditating on a regular basis, so John's adapted philosophy drew me in. It was a major point of our bonding.

If you want to learn about yourself, remove one of your senses. Your response will teach you a wealth of lessons.

These small tests were representative of something much larger than us as individuals. We were in it together, wholeheartedly. The connection we formed from these blind experiments cemented our union as a couple.

My favorite blind experiment fell during a heavy snowstorm while on vacation. We were in a cabin in the middle of the woods with almost two feet of snow outside. It was 2 a.m., and neither one of us could sleep, so I put on a blindfold (to block out light from a small lamppost placed nearby for guests).

John guided me outside slowly, into the deep quiet of the snow. Again, I found myself making assumptions about what I would feel and sense. I thought it would be boring and cold with no sound. What I felt at first was the pure terror of the weight of the forest. I really felt the heaviness of the black night. I told John how I was feeling, and he verbally led me through an immersion in mindfulness. He told me to focus on the sound of the snow.

I didn't know it made such a beautiful, delicate noise when it hit the ground! The "pffts" of the blankets of snow that fell from the branches of the surrounding trees sounded like clouds pitter-pattering. The weight of the trees became comforting, like a blanket surrounding us. The snow kissed my face, one flake after another.

I was fully present for the first time in a long time. It was a relief. I had been anxious for so much of my life. This peace felt like home. John felt like home.

Another experiment led us to make sandwiches together, and I was blindfolded once again. On this particular day, it had been a while since we had done any of our blind experiments, and I was reminded of how intimate it felt. When I "lost" my sight, my world became the size of a dime. He stood

Experiencing the snow with John that night was a
revelatory experience, and one I'll never forget.

next to me, sometimes guiding my hand, and sometimes letting me fumble.
Each time we tried to give each other a kiss, we would miss by miles,
giggling and trying again. It brought us both fully into the present moment.

I read recently that presence is the true meaning of grace. If that is
true, I'm so grateful that grace has brought me here. Finding lessons in
the mundane, truly experiencing the ordinary, can make any moment
exceptional. And those who have met John know he is anything but
ordinary. He teaches me daily to soak up each moment by paying close
attention to all my senses, and finding new perspectives has enriched my
life enormously.

Nature has always been a connector for our relationship. Our first trip
to the ocean together started with some hesitation from John. Being blind
from age sixteen and being from the West, he had never visited the ocean
in person.

He told me he had never seen it when he had sight and had kind of
avoided it because he felt it would be bittersweet now. When I first asked
him about going to the coast, he told me he was worried it would be too
painful for him, because he wouldn't be able to see and experience the

I was thankful to be able to be there the first time John experienced the ocean. This day marked an important moment for us, as it was our first big adventure together in nature.

beauty of the ocean. He was also missing his sense of smell, so he relied mostly on his hearing and touch.

He decided he wanted to try, so we headed to a little coastal town nearby that I had grown up going to. It was the kind of town that had events all year round. It had kite festivals, a car parade down the main drag, and food festivals to celebrate the annual harvests of cranberries and garlic.

Our first stop was a small beach I knew would be mostly empty so John could have some privacy. Before guiding him across the sand, I suggested he remove his shoes and socks. Barefoot, he wiggled his toes in the warm sand. It was a mix of fine sand, small rocks, and dried flora.

We walked together down to the shore. He rolled up his pants and asked me to guide him into the water. He was surprised at how cold it was. He asked if I wouldn't mind giving him some alone time to absorb the experience.

I walked down the beach a bit and sat, watching him. I had gotten permission from him to take photos of him standing there, so I did, and then let him be. After about twenty minutes, he turned around and had a satisfied, peaceful look on his face.

I asked him how it went, and he said it wasn't what he expected. He was pleasantly surprised at the pull of the waves on his ankles and how his toes sunk into the wet sand with each receding ebb current.

He felt the vastness of the water that went on and on. The sound of the tide, the wind, and the gulls all made for a great soundtrack.

That was the start of our adventures in nature.

One of our outings was a trip to the Olympic Peninsula, an area rich with large moss-covered trees and long coastlines. John's friend Bud, who had passed away in 2011, used to own property up near the northwest tip of Washington. Bud's descriptions of centuries-old rainforests, diverse wildlife, and snow-capped mountains were enough to make John want to move there.

We planned on staying in some cabins up near the northeast corner of the Quinault Indian Nation. Along the way, we visited beaches to collect shells and stones. John took a photo of me that is still one of my favorites to this day.

We decided to check out a cedar tree that was described as one of the largest and oldest in the United States. At almost 1,000 years old, it was sure to be an interesting landmark and we wanted to check it out.

Before we drove to the tree, I had looked up the directions; I'm always someone who likes to be prepared. I parked near the start of the trail, or what I thought was the start of the trail, I should say. We later found out there was a parking lot we should have parked in, and that it should have been a "short, easily accessible walk." Apparently, Mother Nature was having a good laugh at us that day, because we most certainly did not have a short or easy walk.

We started the trail, which was covered in thick, raised roots. Holding hands, I tried to guide John and give an audio description of the landscape. I warned him each time we had to "climb" over large boulders or when the landscape became particularly steep. About halfway up, I realized that I might have made a mistake, and maybe this wasn't the correct pathway. But we could hear tourists laughing and talking far up ahead, so I knew we

This is my favorite photo of myself, and I love it all the more because John took it during our trip to the Olympic Peninsula.

were at least headed in the right direction. A part of me felt guilty because I should have been more prepared. But John assured me he wasn't afraid of a little adventure, and we both agreed to keep going.

These were the moments in our relationship that taught me what I needed to know about John. He appeared to be fearless, willing to at least try anything once. He has helped me overcome a lot of my own fears, often by just observing him attempt something, even if he wasn't successful at it.

I was also reminded during these times that I needn't shelter him or feel responsible for his safety. John preferred that I trust him because he trusted himself and knew his own limits.

While I have learned, and am still learning, many lessons related to this, it doesn't stop people from seeing our relationship and John's blindness in a certain light. There have been many times in our relationship where someone will make assumptions about the dynamic that prevails between us. A woman in a grocery store once told me that she was so happy that John had me to help him. She said this in front of him. I remember my eyes widening at her comment, and I said, "We make a great team." I was trying to imply that he helps me, too, and hoped that it came through in my response.

I may appear to help John in very obvious ways, such as how I guide him in public, describe scenery, make food for him, and drive him places. But these are all things that John would be able to find a solution for without me. I know he is grateful to me, but there are also unobservable things that we both assist each other with that hold even more value.

Holding space for each other is a big one. For us, this means listening when one of us is going through a difficult time or feeling anxious about a situation. I am prone to anxiety attacks, and John has taught me things he's learned along the way. He'll hold my hand and encourage me to breathe deeply. We both have a history of trauma in our lives. Sometimes this can be a hindrance for couples if each party hasn't done their own healing. Luckily, each of us has been through therapy or rehab, and we've gleaned coping skills from those experiences. And we aren't perfect, of course. Learning the skills and applying them are two different things, especially when one is having an episode like a panic attack or feeling an intense emotion. And doing things the "wrong" way is a great way to learn for the next time. We've had plenty of those lessons along the way.

By the time we reached the majestic tree, we were sweating and out of breath. We were both a bit cranky, too. The steep, rocky forest floor was a huge challenge for the both of us. When we reached the tree, it took my breath away. I could see it was worth it. I just wish John could also soak up the visual beauty of the ancient giant.

I led him up to the tree, and he put his hand on the bark, trying to take in the enormous diameter of the trunk. He unfolded his white cane and used it to tap the sides as far as it would go each way, upward and sideways. It was possible to take in the tactile quality of the tree in this way, but not fully.

I spotted an opening in the tree and realized we had access to the inside of the tree's trunk.

"Should we try to climb inside?" I asked, feeling brave.

"We've come this far. Let's do it," John said.

We very carefully squeezed through the opening, and the moment we each set foot inside, we realized our mistake. The entire inside of the tree was a mud pit. Our socks and shoes sank into wet ground. As I tried to lift my foot, my shoe came off! I was able to find it again, but by now it was totally soaked.

There was nothing to do but laugh uproariously at this absurd scenario we had put ourselves in. We hugged, and I looked up. The inside of the trunk went up and up. It reminded me of a cathedral with a vaulted ceiling. We snapped a photo, both with goofy grins on our faces. Then we agreed to hightail it out of there to get back to our cabin.

Back at the safe, dry interior of our tiny rental cabin, John suggested he build a fire. He had brought an axe with him, thinking we might need it. A bundle of wood was already at our cabin, which, funnily enough, disappointed John because he had been hoping to use the axe. He approached the owner, asking if he had more wood that John could chop for fun. I really wish I would have been there to see the look on this man's face, who said go for it!

I had brought my camera with me and was excited to capture John's bravery. He carefully placed the pieces on the chopping trunk, and one after another, chopped the wood into smaller pieces. After I took some photos of him, I just sat back with my mouth open, hardly believing what I was seeing.

We headed back to the cabin with an armload of kindling and small logs. He got to work building the fire while I showered to rid myself of the mud from our tree journey.

I came out to a beautiful fire and John relaxing on the nearby bed with his arms behind his head. I would have thought he was sleeping if it weren't for the satisfied smile on his face. That was the look of a proud man. And justifiably so!

On our way home from the trip, the roads were windy and steep. I had borrowed my parents' minivan since I didn't have a car at the time. I wasn't used to driving an automatic. Most of my cars had been manual. I knew how to navigate steep hills with a stick shift by lowering the gear, but an automatic was a different story. I'm sure I relied too heavily on the brakes, and at one point I felt them loosening up. I started getting nervous and commented that maybe we should pull over to let the van rest. Just then, the pedal completely gave way, and I felt it push all the way to the floor.

Trying not to freak out, I remembered what my dad had taught me years ago when I was learning to drive. I had seen a sign a ways back about an upcoming rest stop and thought I would coast until we got to it. I was lucky! The rest stop came up suddenly, and I pulled the emergency brake. As the ground flattened out, we slowed down, and I eased into a parking spot, softly bumping up against the curb.

"Great job!" John exclaimed.

I admit, I was pretty proud of myself for my quick thinking, but honestly, we got lucky with a few of the factors in play.

"Pop open the hood," John said.

"What for?" I stupidly asked.

"So I can check the brake fluid." Of course he knew how to work on cars. There was nothing he couldn't do! The more I learned about John, the more I learned NOT to underestimate him.

I popped the hood, and he asked me to look at the line on the reservoir containing brake fluid. I noticed it was close to empty.

There was a woman nearby, so I asked her if she had extra brake fluid by any chance. She did. At the time, John was still smoking cigarettes, so he traded her a smoke for the bottle.

He told me to get in the car and pump the brakes three times, holding the pedal down on the third pump. Then, he used his multi-tool to open a small valve on the brake calipers, which allowed him to vent any air that had gotten into the brake line. He closed the valve, and I took my foot off the brake. I noticed that the woman and a few other people had started watching John. There was a small crowd taking in what was happening. I laughed that him working on our car had become a bit of a spectacle.

Without my quick maneuver behind the wheel, our luck, and John's knowledge of cars, we probably would have been up the creek. This was just one example of how teamwork laid the foundation of our relationship. These mishaps became kind of a tradition in our relationship. I have an inkling the Universe thought they would be good lessons for us! We took each of them head-on, though it sometimes took a little bickering to get there.

We started calling these little side quests "parking lot dates," as most of them happened in parking lots. The next one happened on our way to a miniature golf date. We stopped to grab something at the store, and when we got back to the car, my key fob wouldn't work. John suggested the battery was most likely dead, so I called around to a hardware store about a half mile from where we were. They told me they carried the type of battery we were looking for, but they were closing in about ten minutes. So we booked it over there, reaching the doors right before they locked them.

It was in the mid 80s that day, so we were both hot, tired, and cranky by the time we got back to the car. We decided to skip our golf outing and grab some dinner to go. We went home and cuddled up with a movie instead.

Another time, I had driven to the store about a mile from our house on my own, which meant going down a very steep hill. If not for the hill, it would have been a pleasant walk. After my shopping, I went to get in the car and found I had a flat tire. Being an older, but new-to-me car, I hadn't checked the supplies in the spare tire well yet. I was annoyed to find it didn't have a tire iron in it. I called John to let him know I was stranded. He told me not to worry, that he'd made that walk many times before we met and would meet me there. He showed up with a socket set and got to work changing the tire, once again saving the day.

Throughout our journey together, I have witnessed John's remarkable abilities, resilience, and creativity in overcoming challenges that many sighted, able-bodied individuals would struggle with.

There have been many times in our relationship that people have doubted John or wondered why I wasn't helping him more. The simple reason is that I don't need to, most of the time. I offer my help, and ninety percent of the time, he says, "Thank you, but I've got it covered." People have their assumptions, and there is nothing we can do about that. If they think I'm neglecting my "poor, blind husband," that's on them. I've had to learn to let go of the judgment of others in so many ways, including how people view our marriage dynamic.

Throughout our journey together, I have witnessed John's remarkable abilities, resilience, and creativity in overcoming challenges that many sighted, able-bodied individuals would struggle with.

By embracing a mindset of inclusivity and discarding preconceived notions, society has an opportunity to recognize the immense potential and incredible talents that exist within people like my husband. Such a shift not only benefits those with disabilities, but also helps foster a more compassionate and understanding world overall, where capabilities are celebrated regardless of physical ability. Ultimately, we can collectively challenge stereotypes and embrace a more inclusive mindset, paving the way for a better future for everyone.

Meeting John's family gave me a glimpse into how John gained his independent, can-do attitude. On a trip to Utah to visit, I observed the confidence that his family members had in John. When he announced that he would barbecue the hot dogs, no one batted an eye. He immediately got to work turning on the grill and gathering the hot dogs, as well as the tongs needed to turn them. He stood, turning them on the grill, effortlessly joking and laughing with everyone. It was heartwarming to see their trust in him and how close he was to his family.

We are both pretty close to our families. We each met the other's family early in our relationship, which was an important meeting. The first time John met my family was at a wedding. I remember thinking how brave he was to attend a family wedding so early on, as we had only been dating about two weeks at that time. The ceremony was a Catholic one, too, so it was a full mass. A full mass ceremony is about an hour long with repeated standing, sitting, and genuflecting (kneeling). I was glad he got to experience a bit of my upbringing. Even though I wasn't a practicing Catholic any longer, it was still a part of who I was. My family loved John right away and were so happy I had found someone who understood me and loved me for me.

The same went for John. Though he wasn't Mormon, his family was, and his upbringing played a big role in who he is today. His parents are kind people with generous hearts. I think we had just gotten engaged right before my first trip to Utah to meet them. It had been almost two years since

John and I had first met. I was terrified to meet everyone, mostly because of my social anxiety. But in the end, I needn't have worried about anything. His large family embraced me immediately. I was able to see where John got his humor and kindness from.

On one of our trips to visit John's family, John and I wanted to check out some local trails. The first one we hiked was relatively easy, but the second one provided one of the greatest lessons our relationship has faced together.

A majority of the trail followed a steep cliff with a running river down below. It was a hot, dry day, the red dust of the trail kicking up as we made our way. I was wearing a backpack, and to navigate the path safely, John was holding onto the strap of my pack. I described the trail as we went along, and most of the ground was covered with roots and rocks, which made for serious tripping hazards. Not exactly a blind-friendly hike!

The trail ended up being about five and half miles round trip, with hot springs at the end. When we reached the hot springs, we were both a bit cranky but didn't want to disappoint each other and tried our best to keep smiles on our faces. The surroundings were stunning, but I was being bitten by horseflies and John was grossed out by the slimy moss in the pools. His niece took some cute photos of us—the smiles on our faces are authentic in that we were happy thinking the other was happy. It wasn't until much later that we both fessed up to it being a trail we would rather skip in the future! It reminded me of one of our favorite stories, "The Gift of the Magi."

Yes, it was sweet that we didn't want to ruin the experience for each other, but it was a great reminder for us to communicate better in the future.

That trek taught us a lot about each other in many ways. Our mental endurance was challenged, but we remained kind to and patient with each other. I can't say it's always like this in our relationship. There are moments of projection and tension just like any normal partnership. But through experiences like this, we've learned how to value our feelings and share them with each other without hurting one another. Most of the time, it's not easy. But marriage isn't a conveyor belt that runs automatically. It's more of an obstacle course. And we approach those trials together. Holding hands through adversity has made our bond tighter.

Something that has been different from any other relationship I've had is that, instead of viewing our conflicts as head-to-head showdowns, we try to view conflicts as problems that we can work on and solve together. You could call it a riddle to decode as a team. This has made us stronger in all aspects.

CHAPTER 6

Back to the Sawdust: Starting Over Again

—————— JOHN ——————

My relationship with Anni was rocky in the beginning, but even so, I felt intense sparks between us. At the time, our relationship was a mixed-ability relationship, meaning I had a disability and she, for all we knew, did not. This was before her chronic health problems started really affecting her quality of life. My blindness made things especially complex, with more added challenges than would have been the case for an able-bodied couple.

In the past, I had difficulty in my romantic relationships. They ended because of various reasons, but sometimes it was due to my blindness. It can be hard for sighted partners not to be seen by a blind partner. Some people like feedback about their beauty and miss the validation of this. Anni had a little bit of a hard time with this in the beginning but also told me that she appreciated my ability to see her differently than her other partners. At one point, she told me that I was the only person who really saw her because I was only seeing her heart and her mind. And I could see her with my hands, you could say!

Something I really like about being blind is that I cannot judge others based on their appearance. You know the saying, don't judge a book by its cover? Well, I can't see the cover, I only see stories.

This makes life far more interesting to me.

I had a few long-term relationships before I met Anni. I had even been engaged twice to two different people. When I think back on these partnerships, they didn't feel like they were "meant to be." I was young and inexperienced. I think the reason it didn't work out those other times was

I hope my blindness adds to the poetry behind each piece, just like any artist's story adds to the beauty of their creation.

because we realized it wasn't what we wanted. We were together out of convenience, not love. But my past relationships weren't without lessons. I learned that I had been selfish in my partnerships in a lot of ways and was only invested in myself. I think I needed to have some time to grow and learn who I was before I was ready for any kind of truly serious relationship.

When we first met, I immediately knew how kind her heart was, and it wasn't long before I recognized how talented she was in so many ways, including her cooking.

I wanted to prove to myself that I could live independently and not have to rely on someone else to survive. I needed to stay out of trouble and live successfully on my own.

With Anni, I've experienced so much personal growth, and our relationship is fueled by genuine love and connection. Even though I can't see her, I know how beautiful she is inside. When I met Anni, I felt like I found a kindred spirit. She had a charming, bright presence. The energy she expressed when helping the kids from the shelter was nurturing, and I loved how encouraging she was as they worked together on the piano that first week. Her quirky sense of humor matched with my wit has kept us laughing all these years. We've spent many a night giggling to the point of tears together, our humor bouncing back and forth like a tennis match.

Anni's level of empathy for others is profound. She cares deeply about fairness and equality in the world, and she hurts for others who are in pain.

Our connection to nature is something we have in common. We can stand in the middle of the forest together quietly soaking up the beauty and sounds. She has helped me over the years find a wider view of the world. All the people she's introduced me to, new types of food, music, concerts, art, ideas, these are all things that have broadened my perspective.

When we first met, I immediately knew how kind her heart was, and it wasn't long before I recognized how talented she was in so many ways, including her cooking. What a bonus for me, because I love to eat! And even though I can't see her art, I know she is a gifted artist. People often ask how I know she is a good artist. Seeing can be done in different ways. She makes tactile art that I can feel and touch.

When we first met, Anni was a photographer and painter. These were mediums that were inaccessible to me, and I knew it bothered her that she couldn't share her art with me. As our relationship progressed, Anni was determined to learn new creative methods so she could share her projects with me. She started learning new art techniques such as sculpture, embroidery, wool felting, miniature building, wood carving, and sewing. This allowed me to explore how talented she is, and it brought us closer together. We also share our creative ideas and our techniques.

Being disabled means sometimes needing more assistance than an able-bodied partner would need. Luckily, Anni understood this part and is naturally a nurturing person. She likes to tell me she is my biggest fan and this shows up in the ways she helps me throughout my life. She not only guides me in public, but she helps me at home, assists me by identifying species of wood in the woodshop, and gives me new perspectives on life's philosophies. She now also runs our business and all our social media.

In the winter of 2013, fourteen years after my attempt, I graduated from the piano school. After I graduated, I decided to start my own business immediately. While I'd still be in school, my mentor, Rick, and I hatched a plan. I would work under him for a while after graduating, and then I'd buy the business from him. Most of my work was assisting Rick, who continued to mentor me until I purchased his piano-repair tools from him in 2013.

To start rebuilding pianos, I had to first obtain all the parts and equipment I needed, which would require a considerable investment. Anni organized a fundraiser for me that raised $16,000. The fundraiser was successful because Anni is a whiz at social media, though she is very modest and insists she's not. She got the exposure that I needed and word of it was broadcast on the local news. It even got picked up by TV news in Seattle, which eventually got onto the *Huffington Post*, and from the *Huffington Post* to a newspaper in Mumbai, India.

She literally made me world famous in a short amount of time. What I didn't know at the time was that, with Anni steering the ship, this was just the beginning of my "fame." She doesn't like me saying this, but nobody would know who I am without her hard work, dedication, and loyalty to me. She even designed my piano business logo, turning the *F* in my last name into a music note. The name of my business was John Furniss, Piano Service.

My piano workshop would often have at least two or three pianos in various stages of repair in it. I worked on spinets, uprights, and grands. My favorite kind to work on were grand pianos, the access to all the parts was much easier to reach. Uprights were a pain to deal with, particularly spinets, which were the smaller instruments. Every time I knew I had to work on those small pianos another word that started with *S* went through my mind (hint: it wasn't "super")!

I had several benches around the shop, each of them built with a specific purpose in mind. For instance, one bench was dedicated to repairing piano keys, another was for repairing upright piano actions, and one was for grands. Various tools hung on the walls. There were special jigs, a sander, a drill press, as well as shelves with dozens of plastic tubs containing various special parts for pianos. There were thousands and thousands of vital components housed in these containers.

I had a mobile cabinet full of large spools of various sizes of wire designed specifically for restringing pianos. On the top of the cabinet was a post for mounting the spool and a clamp to run the wire through to make it easier to control while stringing.

When I worked on pianos, I generally leaned over the top or leaned the large instrument on its side for access. Most of the time when working on the action (a.k.a. all the moving parts inside), it would be taken out of the piano and put on one of the benches. After the new parts had been put on, I had to readjust the action to get it properly recalibrated.

With an upright, recalibration had to be done inside the piano. With a grand, it was done on a bench. There was a large hoist on the ceiling, with a metal hook and straps to hoist the iron plate out of a piano to be sanded and repainted. The plates weigh anywhere between 200–500 pounds, sometimes even more than that.

My business did well in the beginning, mostly because Rick had a lot of connections and Anni helped me with social media and advertising.

Working with pianos was not easy. They are very heavy, often dirty, and complex. A piano is very much a machine before it is an instrument. The inner workings of a piano have always reminded me of a clock. A piano's "action" has 7,200 parts, and around 4,500 of those parts are moving parts.

Working on a piano can be tedious, repetitive work. Since a piano has eighty-eight keys, that also means it has at least eighty-eight of every single part, if not more. If you have to do something once, you must do it at least eighty-seven more times, except for strings. On average, there are 220 strings in a piano, and restringing was my favorite task.

I loved piano work because it was science, mostly geometry and physics. As I've mentioned, I'm a lifelong science nerd! I learned about acoustics and scaling a piano, which means calculating what string length and diameter you need to achieve a particular note in the proper sonic frequency. Despite the setbacks I encountered during my piano business days, I took great pride in my piano work. Many told me that my work was the equal of any sighted technician they had ever seen. I pride myself on getting things done as perfectly as I can.

Restringing was engaging, I had to measure the old strings with a talking micrometer because the exact diameter of the string was critical. After I measured the strings with a micrometer and marked down where the different sizes changed. I would remove all the old, rusty strings and tuning pins. Then, I had to clean everything up.

One of the things that I found interesting is that every piano has a set of bass strings specifically made for that one piano. The way that you have the factory match new round piano strings is that you lay a large piece of butcher paper across all the strings with windings, tape it down, and then use sandpaper to make holes where all of the wire windings end on each string. It's almost like a stencil, and then you send that piece of paper in with a couple of the strings as samples, and the factory will make you a whole new set of custom strings for that particular piano. I loved learning little tricks of the trade like that.

Replacing hammers was interesting. Several things needed to be done to the hammers before they were ready to put on the piano. And there was a tool that made each step very accurate.

After a couple years, business began to slow down and I was beginning to "see the light" that this work might not be for me, or good for the long term. As an artist at heart, I am creative and enjoy variety in life. The monotony of piano work was weighing on my spirit.

It weighed on me physically, too. A lot of the time, I had to have my arms out in front of me for many hours, making small adjustments. This was hard on me because I had broken my back three times, which led to intense pain. I would sometimes do other activities as a sort of physical therapy to help me build up my back muscles. Walking and working in the garden helped ease some of my pain.

With piano work, the only real variety was when you got an older piano with a weird design that wasn't in use anymore. That always made it interesting! I also loved finding old items inside the pianos—things like baseball cards, old magazines, and utility bills. I collected these. I found an Alfred Hitchcock *Reader's Digest* issue and one time I found a small plastic green skeleton. Dead bugs and mouse droppings were very common, so it was important to wear rubber gloves.

I was thankful to all the people who'd helped me achieve this dream, but sometimes we find out too late that our dreams aren't always what we thought they'd be. Holding onto this one when it simply wasn't working out was starting to drag me down. I reminded myself that if I hadn't gone through the piano program, I never would have met Anni.

I rebuilt pianos with Rick until the winter of 2014, when I realized piano rebuilding was just not for me any longer. The repetitiveness and the struggle to find customers was starting to bother me, and it was making me very depressed. It was hard for me to face that fact because I had devoted so much time and effort to coming up from Salt Lake City to learn how to rebuild pianos and find another direction for my life. I'd thought this would be my calling. But, in my heart, I knew I needed to move on. I was thankful

Here, I'm holding a bowl I made from that old Chickering piano.

to all the people who'd helped me achieve this dream, but sometimes we find out too late that our dreams aren't always what we thought they'd be. Holding onto this one when it simply wasn't working out was starting to drag me down. I reminded myself that if I hadn't gone through the piano program, I never would have met Anni. Maybe closing this one door would lead to the next adventure. I like to say God never farts without opening a window, ha!

I remember the very piano that made me decide to quit once and for all. It was a 1929 Fisher grand, on which someone had gotten the bright idea to put a bunch of epoxy around the tuning pins. It took a week to clean all of it off to get the plate ready to be repainted. At the end of that rebuild, I decided to stop rebuilding pianos with Rick. I wasn't quite sure if I was going to continue rebuilding or not. I still had all the tools, and I think

I was trying to convince myself that I wanted to stay in the business but work independently.

I officially shut down my business in 2015. It was very difficult for both Anni and me when I stopped working on pianos. She encouraged my decision because she could see how much of a toll continuing to force myself into the job was taking on me. Fortunately, she got two new jobs and supported us for a couple of years after that.

In 2016, we moved to the house we live in now. I finally decided that I was done with the piano stuff and Anni knew that my true skills and passion were in woodworking. Knowing that the lathe has always been my favorite tool to work with, she bought me one for my birthday in 2016. I was eager to start using it.

At the time, I had a large old Chickering upright piano that was beyond help, so I decided to disassemble it carefully and use the wood from the case and to make handcrafted pieces from the lid. It worked out very well. I made some nice bowls using the wood from that piano. I still have a few back posts—the large support post that can be seen on the back of an upright piano—floating around, and I make stuff out of them now and then.

The first time I made a bowl on the lathe turned out to be an interesting experience. Though I had been using the lathe for many years before this, I had never made a bowl. The big difference is where the tool rest is. That is a part of the lathe you put your chisel on, and you use it as leverage when carving. With a bowl, there is a large space between the tool rest and the work surface, so your chisel can be pulled between the two if you aren't careful. Every project I had done on the lathe up to that point did not have that particular danger.

Watch John's documentary via this code.

When I started the first bowl, a friend of ours named Chris Martin, who is a documentarian, asked me if he could film me while I was at work. He came over on the first day that I was working on the bowl and filmed the process. Over the next couple days, he ended up making a wonderful documentary. The day after he left, I was working on the bowl but using the

My shop is full of woods of all shapes, sizes, and varieties. Sometimes, I need a bit of help sorting them, but I can often identify them by feel.

wrong chisel for the wrong job. I was resting my finger on top of the chisel where it definitely should not have been, and the chisel dug into the wood and twisted around, which smashed my finger between the side of the chisel and the tool rest. It popped like a grape!

I left a trail of blood like a wounded cowboy in a John Wayne movie. It was one of those things that happens so quickly that it didn't even seem to hurt at first. My first thought after I moved my finger to make sure the tendons were okay was, *Dammit, it will be weeks before I finish this project*! My finger seemed fine, so I touched the tip to make sure the nerve was okay. I still had feeling in it, which seemed like a good sign. I knew all that I'd need would probably be a little needlepoint (a.k.a. stitches).

Pretty soon, I began dripping blood everywhere. It was on my face and all over my hands and pouring out of my fist, which I had wrapped around my finger. I left the shop and went to the back door of the house and shouted, "Anni, I hurt myself!"

When she came to the door, she opened it and saw the extent of the damage. I'm sure it was quite a horrifying sight to see. She told me to come inside. Understandably, she was very upset.

She was starting to have a bit of a panic attack, and said, "You need to sit down, you are going into shock."

I said, "Sweetie, I am doing fine. I think you are the one going into shock."

We were able to help each other get everything figured out. She brought me a handful of paper towels, and I wrapped them around my finger. Then, we went to the emergency room. I needed eleven stitches, and it took eight weeks to heal up. During that recovery period, I carefully tended to my wound and deeply contemplated the concept of "don't put your finger there, you idiot!" which has become a guiding philosophy of my life.

After recovering, I finished what we have come to call The Blood Bowl and gave it to Anni as a gift. It still sits in our living room as a centerpiece, where it serves as a useful reminder that I should be fully mindful in my work.

Our new place had a garage in the back, which I'd turned into my woodshop. All the benches I'd bought when I was rebuilding pianos were on heavy-duty casters, so they came with me to our new house. They were built for working on pianos, so they were sturdily made, nice, and flat. Most of the tools I purchased while working on pianos were woodworking tools, so I was able to transfer them to my new work and passion.

The next bowl I worked on was quite large—10" x 10". Most of the wood in that bowl came from the Chickering upright piano I had taken apart. It was the first of many projects to be made from the wood I salvaged from that piano. There was a nice symbolism to this, I think—making new things from the leftovers of my old business.

It felt good to keep my hands busy and feel like my life had a new direction. I wasn't sure where that direction would lead me, but that all changed when Anni's mom asked me to make her a small jewelry dish to put her rings in. After I made it, Anni took a photo and put it on her Facebook page. Within twenty-four hours I had orders for fourteen of those dishes.

It seemed I had my answer. Anni quickly started an Etsy page for me, and we sold several things there.

Anni had been doing art shows and festivals on her own over the years, and that year it looked like I would be joining her. It was the beginning of our life as an artist couple. At the time, I was still playing around with the idea of getting a regular job. I was working with the local chapter of vocational rehab. During one of our meetings, Anni showed the counselor photos of my wooden creations.

My counselor looked at both of us and asked, "Why don't you do this? You are so gifted. I know people would buy your things."

And she was right. It was then that I gave up finding a nine-to-five and focused on making things in my woodshop.

Because I wasn't good at social media or anything computer-related, Anni took care of that part of our business. Due to her physical challenges, I felt bad that I couldn't do much to help, but it was something she loved to do. She's not only good at social media and promotion, but she also told me she enjoys doing it. She said that, since she is my number one fan, it makes it even easier for her to promote me.

That year, I did my first art festival. It was an exciting time, and I made many things to prepare for it: bowls, trays, rolling pins, and canisters. It was fun to let my creativity shine.

In my process, I try not to make items with the same designs. I have a very visual imagination and can picture what I want to do clearly in my mind. I like to say I have a computer design program in my head. I can change it as I need until I have the image ready. When I'm ready to create, my hands build the design. Then, I get to hand someone the finished piece and they can see what I see. It's a rewarding experience that, for me, is almost like a visual release.

Really, the only difference between sighted and blind woodworkers (other than sight) is the way we measure. I only have one adaptive tool in my whole shop, which is my Rotomatic. It's also one of the simplest tools in my woodshop. It opens up the entire craft of woodworking for me.

I give most of my tools nicknames in my woodshop. I use a lathe ("Kathleen Turner"), sliding miter saw ("Blue"), a planer ("The Banshee"), a large standalone belt sander ("Colonel Sanders"), various parting tools ("The Moses Family"), and my favorite chisels ("Big Jake" and "Excalibur"). As a whole, I call my chisels "The Carver Family." The other tools I use that don't have nicknames are a manual drill, a table saw, a ratchet screwdriver, a handsaw, a biscuit cutter, clamps, and various hand chisels.

Sharing my art with people at the festivals was incredibly gratifying for me. Hearing their reactions and getting feedback in person filled my cup. It eased a lot of the sadness I had been feeling for months. I was finally pointed the right way, and contributing to our household, which made me feel good about myself.

We kept very busy that year doing festivals and even an open studio tour where people could come watch me in my woodshop. They could observe me in my natural habitat! The festivals were hit and miss with how much we sold, but we always left them feeling good about meeting people and talking with them about our art.

Preparing for an art festival can be very time-consuming. First, we made our art pieces, which takes a lot of physical and mental energy. Then, Anni organized everything we needed for the day or days into big plastic tubs. Tablecloths, signs, card displays, and our artwork all fit into the tubs. Larger items like canopies, tables, rugs, chairs, and shelves would be strapped to the top of our small car. We liked to say that Anni was the brains, and I was the brawn. She would do all the festival scheduling, planning, advertising, social media, and packing in addition to making her own pieces for the shows. I would craft my inventory and be responsible for carrying heavy items and packing the car. I jokingly called myself her pack mule.

Then it was set-up time when we arrived at the venue. This was always a chaotic time, with all the other artists and vendors bustling around us. Anni would carry what she could, while guiding me to our space while I was also carrying something large. I'm sure we were quite the sight! We were a parade, and not always graceful. There were times we bumped into other people or dropped items we were carrying. This was when our practice of teamwork and patience came in handy.

Carrying the items to our designated exhibit space was just the beginning. With that accomplished, we'd get to work setting up the canopy or canopies, as sometimes we had two. We'd set up the tables and shelving. Anni, having done a practice setup in our living room of everything, would know just where things were to be placed on the day of the event.

While I tried to stay out of the way as much as I could, she would lay out the tablecloths, set up the signs, and arrange the art. I helped her hang up her larger paintings along the sides of the canopy. Some of them were as big as 4' x 4'.

Once the event began, we were lucky if it was busy. This meant I got to start my show and tell. And then if someone loved my art enough to want to buy it, that brought a whole new level of happiness. Once, a professional magician bought a wand I had made! It's a satisfying thing to get feedback on things I've created with my own hands. I know Anni feels the same.

We'd start seeing repeat collectors at our shows and knew some people by name. They'd bring their dogs to visit us, and if we'd remembered to bring treats, we offered them to their pups. It was nice to build a community, of sorts.

Then, there were the failed festivals. There were days that we would sit at our booth, exhibiting all our wares, but selling nothing. People would walk by, glance at us, but then keep on walking. It was disheartening. Sometimes people would say rude things about our art. "I could make that," or "The seams on this need to be neater," were some things we heard. Being an artist and sharing your handmade creations with the public means you need to build a thick skin. People say the darndest things!

It was around this time of doing the art festival circuit that Anni encouraged me to share my story more. I was at a point in my life that I felt ready to authentically share what I had been through. This meant being vulnerable in ways I didn't often show people.

I had randomly shared my story over the years to anyone who would listen, but it was out of a craving for attention. Up until then, the way I told my tale was a victim's, woe-is-me perspective instead of a survivor story. Now that I had "done the work," as Anni liked to say, I was ready to share it in an empowering way that I hoped could help others.

I started slowly. Anni and I began by giving talks in local elementary schools, where I could help children learn how to interact with blind people. We taught them about gaining consent of a blind person, to never grab them to guide them, but to ask them if they needed help. The intention of these blindness-awareness talks was to dispel fears that children might have about disabled people who might look different from themselves or most people they knew.

Eventually these talks transformed into deeper messages to older students about mental health, bullying, and suicide awareness. I have now done many of these talks over the years, sometimes to large auditoriums of kids. I always hope I make a difference, since I never heard anyone speak about these types of issues when I was that age. I can't know for sure, but it might have made a difference for me.

As our relationship progressed, Anni encouraged me to access the deeper parts of myself. It hasn't been easy, but it's been worth it.

For years, I would tell my suicide survival story in a very matter-of-fact manner, without feeling the magnitude of how my attempt truly affected me and those around me. When I met Anni, something I noticed right away was that she experienced the world through emotions. I am a very logically minded person, and for years was detached from my feelings, especially regarding my trauma. As our relationship progressed, Anni encouraged me to access the deeper parts of myself. It hasn't been easy, but it's been worth it. The first school talk Anni and I did together was at an elementary school. Her friend was a teacher there and invited us to speak to a class. We spoke to the young children about what blindness is and how to interact with people who are blind. After this experience, we caught a bug. The bug was spreading awareness about things important to us. This included disability, mental health, and art.

As I became more comfortable talking about the traumas I had experienced, it felt important that I share my story with others, specifically young people. When I thought about the bullying that I had experienced and the way it made me feel, it compelled me more than ever to want to speak to middle school and high school kids. I wanted to offer support to those suffering at the hands of bullies and offer insight to those who were inflicting pain onto others. Perhaps my hope to reach kids engaging in bullying behavior is based out of idealism, but even if I help just one kid see the harm they are causing, it all feels worth it. Victims and bullies can be two sides of the same coin. Often, the bully started out as the victim. By engaging in open and nonjudgmental conversations, I hope to encourage them to see things from the perspective of their victims, enabling them to connect with the feelings of those they have hurt.

The next two years were full of a lot of hustle and bustle. We'd only have a couple weeks between festivals, and this meant rarely taking a day off. We had to use every day to make new items to sell. If it weren't for the time constraints, it would have been a bit more enjoyable; as it was, it was very challenging for both of us.

My favorite types of events were open studio tours, in which we literally opened our house to the public. Anni set up her live painting demonstration in the living room while I worked in my woodshop out back. People walked through the front door, watched Anni do her thing and then walked out the back door to watch me at the lathe. We have a little nook off our kitchen that Anni set up as a gift shop to sell our pieces. These two-day events were a great way for me to show people how I used my tools.

I loved interacting with the community and talking with people. I hoped that I was opening people's minds and changing perceptions about blindness. We would sometimes have around 200 people come through over the course of a weekend.

The community we live in is very supportive of artists. There is a lot of public art, and tactile art too. A couple times, Anni and I have gone around our town, finding as much three-dimensional art as we could. Near us there are many sculptures, artists' benches, petroglyphs, and murals. Anni describes the murals to me.

This was a whole new world for me. Anni had been part of the art community for many years in the town we earlier lived in. Everywhere we went we would run into people that knew her or knew of her. It's funny to me that now I'm the one who is more often recognized out in public, because it used to be Anni who got all the attention. Anni was heavily invested in community events for many years. She says they gave her a sense of purpose. Because of this, her circle of friends and fellow volunteers called her The Mayor of Vancouver because of how many events she organized.

It seemed everywhere we went, someone knew her. So it was funny to me that now I was the one in the limelight!

Art should evoke a feeling. Sometimes that feeling is anger, sadness, or even a memory.

It was confusing for me sometimes when we ran into people that knew Anni. She would introduce me to so many people that it was hard to keep track. I only heard voices, so I sometimes pretended I knew who I was talking to, so I wouldn't seem rude. This is why it's always a good idea to tell a blind person who you are when you approach them, even if you've met them before.

Anni's health started to decline again, probably due to working a regular office job and a nanny job on top of all the art festivals we were doing. I knew it was stressful for her, and I felt guilty that I couldn't do more for her. When Anni suggested one day that she wanted to quit her day job, I was apprehensive. On one hand, I wanted her to be able to focus on what she truly loved, which is her art. But I also doubted myself and my ability to sell enough of my art to make a difference.

It was a struggle at first. We had to get a lot of assistance from food banks, and Anni applied for some artist grants, and to my surprise, we were able to get a couple of them. We worked in the unfamiliar territory of trying to support ourselves as professional artists. There is a whole other level of complexity working as an artist and trying to make most of your income from it.

You have to strike an emotional chord in someone so that they become willing to purchase a piece of art from someone that may be a painting costing several hundred or even thousands of dollars. Some people don't understand that artwork costs that much because each piece can take a very long time to make. It's not just that—the buyer is also paying for someone's experience, their techniques, their knowledge. Appreciating the artist's whole story is just as important as appreciating their creations.

There have been comments sometimes from strangers on the internet saying things like, "Do you charge that much because you're blind?" It's a rude thing to say, yes. But it also doesn't consider the extra patience, effort,

Here, I'm attaching a faceplate to a wood blank, preparing it for the lathe, circa 2022.

Preparing to turn a cannister made of SpectraPly® wood.

A collaborative keepsake box made of black walnut, turned by me and hand painted by Anni (fitting, as Honeybee is my go-to pet name for her)

Here I am using a bench grinder to sharpen my chisels.
These days, I typically use a sander instead.

I always keep a stockpile of wood to use for projects.

A salad bowl made of padauk and ash.

A collaborative piece made of black walnut, turned by me
and hand painted by Anni.

A jewelry tray made of padauk and yellowheart.

A mortar and pestle made of ash. On this, I used a charring technique to create a unique coloring.

My "crown jewel," the table I built after
breaking my back.

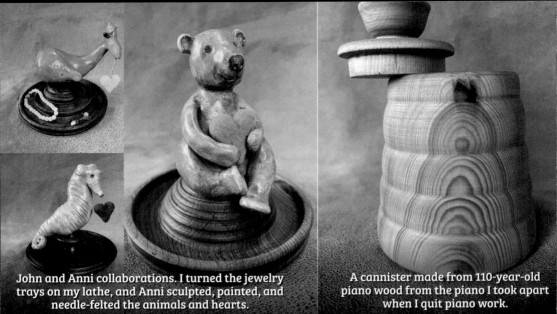

John and Anni collaborations. I turned the jewelry trays on my lathe, and Anni sculpted, painted, and needle-felted the animals and hearts.

A cannister made from 110-year-old piano wood from the piano I took apart when I quit piano work.

Here, I use a scraper chisel while turning a smartphone speaker amplifier on the lathe.

Here, I'm using friction to char a small piece of wood, causing smoke to billow out.

A yarn bowl we made. I turned the bowl and
Anni used a rotary tool to create the yarn cutout design.

A salad bowl made of padauk and yellowheart wood.

My first bowl.

A large bowl made from the Chickering piano I was gifted.

A collaboration. Anni sculpted and painted the whale and balloon, and I made the wooden base.

I often feel the tips of my chisels to be sure I'm using the right one for the job.
Photo by Nolan Calisch.

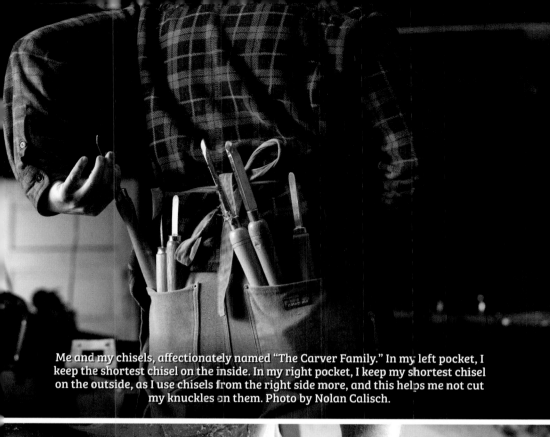

Me and my chisels, affectionately named "The Carver Family." In my left pocket, I keep the shortest chisel on the inside. In my right pocket, I keep my shortest chisel on the outside, as I use chisels from the right side more, and this helps me not cut my knuckles on them. Photo by Nolan Calisch.

While turning, I use my hands to feel the grain and the changing shape. Photo by Nolan Calisch.

Me outside my woodshop.
Photo by Nolan Calisch

Here, I'm feeling the grooves I've cut into this piece.
Photo by Nolan Calisch.

I like to apply a finish to my pieces so they are protected and will stay beautiful for years to come. I almost always use a clear coat of a wax blend, which really lets the wood's natural beauty shine through.
Photo by Nolan Calisch.

A salad bowl made of padauk and ash.

Here, I'm preparing to sand a piece on my belt sander.
Photo by Nolan Calisch.

Here, I'm turning a bowl made of padauk and ash.
Photo by Nolan Calisch.

and hard work it takes me to complete my pieces. Artists, sighted or not, should be paid for their craft. I hope my blindness adds to the poetry behind each piece, just like any artist's story adds to the beauty of their creation.

Art should evoke a feeling. Sometimes that feeling is anger, sadness, or even a memory. Sometimes that feeling is peaceful, happy, or loving. I love the quote by the educator Dr. César Cruz. He says, "Art should comfort the disturbed and disturb the comfortable."

We each get different things from viewing, or in my case, feeling or hearing art. We're never going to perceive art the same way, or through the same lens. Our life's experiences, how we communicate, how we understand the world, these are all factors that influence our relationships with a work of art, a song, or a poem.

My hope is that when someone sees or holds my art, they are not thinking, "This is a nice piece for a blind guy." I hope they are remembering my story, too. I hope a piece of my legacy is captured, even in small ways, in that bowl.

CHAPTER 7

I See You

ANNI

John and I moved in together in 2013, about a year after we met. A good friend of mine told me the house next door to hers was available for rent. It was in kind of rough shape, but the rent was really low. My friend, who would be our neighbor, was also an artist and was involved in the community, so that made the decision to move there a lot easier.

At the time we moved, John was trying to get a small piano-repair business up and running. His piano-repair mentor, Rick, was selling equipment, and John wanted to buy it to start his own venture. But it was going to require a fair chunk of money. John had mentored under Rick for two years, and they'd had a plan for John to buy the business from him once he finished his mentorship.

I got to work raising funds for John so he could purchase the piano-repair equipment he needed to start his business. The materials and equipment he was purchasing included dozens of different kinds of tools, parts, specialty workbenches, and even salvaged vintage parts that were no longer available and hadn't been manufactured for at least fifty years. Some of the tools were unique to working on pianos and some had even been built by John's mentor Rick. There was a set of jigs Rick built to make it easier for blind people to install new hammers on grand pianos. Hammers are the felt-covered blocks of wood that hit the strings of a piano to make sound when the keys are pressed. John helped him refine these jigs as they were being finished.

Because fundraising was a passion of mine, and I had years of experience doing it, it was familiar territory. I started a Kickstarter campaign where donors received gifts for different levels of contributions. I put out a press release to local and national papers, magazines, news stations, and radio stations. I started posting regularly on Facebook, which was the only social

We both believe in leading with love, and treating others with kindness, empathy, and compassion. These philosophies are our moral compass.

media platform we were using at the time. I posted every day, sharing a new fact about John each time. I shared how John's interest in piano rebuilding began, and stories about his love of working on cars. I posted photos of John when he was younger and of him working on pianos. John's blindness appealed to people's curiosity, and they appreciated his determination.

I had a deep love for the community where I was born and raised and had done a lot of fundraising for events and causes over the years. This fundraiser quickly became my main focus for a couple months. My love for John and his dreams fueled my late nights and hours spent sending out press releases, making social media posts, and gathering donated items to give away as incentives. It was a real community affair; our friends, family and fellow artists pitched in to help spread the word.

John's fundraiser eventually reached as far as India, and he was on the local news a couple times. We were able to raise a little over $16,000 for him to purchase the equipment and start renting a space for his shop.

His shop was about a mile away from our new home, and he was able to walk there every day. For a while, things felt really good, and his business was doing well. At the time, I was attending art school, showing my art in local galleries, and working at our local food co-op.

John continued to be a muse for me and inspired my creativity. Shortly after we moved in together, John knocked over one of my favorite Buddha sculptures (I had a small collection), a beautiful marble one. At the time, I thought little of it until an assignment in my painting class made me dig a little deeper. Our job was to create two paintings. The theme was "The One and The Many." As I sat in my backyard trying to find something that inspired me, the Buddha head kept creeping into my thoughts. The head that was once whole was now lying in three pieces, waiting to be glued back together. I had my subject.

Spilled drinks and broken dishes are a common occurrence in our house, almost daily. It's something I've gotten used to, living with a blind person. Because it became a tradition in our routine, I started taking it for granted, and quite frankly, expecting it. But this time, there was something very symbolic about the broken marble face. Symbolism is such a powerful tool in our lives, one I feel is overlooked time and again. It sometimes doesn't occur to me until it's slapping me in the face, telling me to wake up and listen. This time I was listening.

John still lives with the physical scars from his suicide attempt, which aren't noticeable until given closer inspection; they include a crack on his temple that I've always found intriguing. And because the nerves in his eyelids were destroyed, he always has his eyes closed. Not unlike the Buddha, it has been said many times by people that John appears to be reaching for nirvana. This is something that first attracted me to him. His dimples might have helped, too! John's sense of peace and gentleness manifest on his face and in his body language.

Sometimes, it takes being completely broken to create a new life.

As a blind person, he must be mindful of every step he takes; every movement of his body must be completely intentional. He embodies a mentality of awareness and a be-here-now attitude.

Sometimes, it takes being completely broken to create a new life.

Renewal and rebirth are themes in religions all over the world, for good reason, I believe. When something is destroyed beyond recognition, there are two choices: give up or rebuild. The fork in the road is a difficult one to face, but it forces a choice upon us, even after great trauma. This brings to mind on old cliché: when one door closes, another one opens. Or in John's case, when his eyes were permanently closed, he was involuntarily compelled to make a decision.

Since meeting John over eleven years ago, I've learned so much about the practical, emotional, and spiritual aspects of blindness. People have repeatedly said to me that John is so lucky to have me to care for him. This makes me laugh, because John's independence is something he has fought for and worked hard for since his suicide attempt. He is no victim, and his strength is far more powerful than his loss of sight. He is a symbol of brokenness and destruction. And he has taught me that there is light even amid darkness.

Eventually, John's business started struggling. Finding people who wanted their pianos repaired proved to be very difficult. He didn't do a lot of tuning because, as he admitted himself, he wasn't very good at it.

Tuners often have musical backgrounds, and John didn't have that. He was more mechanically than musically inclined, and so was more interested in repairing pianos than tuning them. However, this was a detriment to his business. Most people just need their pianos tuned, while repairing can be very expensive, sometimes upwards of $7,000 or more. Not everyone is willing to pay that kind of money to fix their family piano. He was depressed at the time and blamed himself for his piano business not being successful, but there weren't many people willing to pay thousands of dollars to rebuild their pianos.

We were struggling financially, trying to stay afloat with the few repair jobs he could get and my mostly part-time job that I had while I attended school. I sold my art when I could, and this helped a little too.

This time in our life felt like one long struggle. John was battling some demons of his own. He was still drinking at this time, and his drinking was out of control. I knew his history with addiction made self-medicating his go-to coping mechanism.

He was also feeling creatively suffocated. Thousands of piano mechanisms meant thousands of adjustments, often doing the same action over and over again for hours. For someone as artistically minded as John, this was stifling.

He became increasingly more depressed.

John's epilepsy was not being managed, especially with him drinking, so there were nights I would wake to him having a grand mal seizure. These were terrifying for me to watch and painful for him to endure. When he had a seizure, he would bite his tongue, blood appearing at his mouth. His face would turn a scary pale blue, and every time he had one, I worried this would be the one that would steal him from me. His neurologist emphasized to us the importance of stopping these seizures. John had one of the most dangerous forms of epilepsy, which were mostly nocturnal episodes that happened while he slept.

Eventually, he did stop drinking. He understood it was consumption of alcohol that contributed to his seizures. I'm sure losing his main coping mechanism was not only difficult mentally, but the withdrawal symptoms were physically awful for him. We both struggled with different addictions throughout our lives. I knew all too well what giving up alcohol felt like, though not to the extreme it was for him.

Because he had moved to Washington, attended piano repair school, had been the recipient of a large fundraiser, and then opened his business, he felt a lot of pressure to stay in the piano field. And try, he did. I helped him promote the business, and he did try tuning pianos a few times, but it took him much longer than other tuners. My heart hurt for him because he had worked so hard to get where he was.

I felt in my heart of hearts that John was supposed to move onto something else. I gingerly brought this subject up several times, but at first, he said he wanted to hang in there. I was supportive and didn't want to discourage him.

I also understood what it was like feeling the pressure of your career weighing on your shoulders I had been a photographer for more than ten years. I started out doing artistic photography, and then moved onto doing a lot of community photos. It was common for me to be seen at events throughout town documenting people and activities. I loved every moment of it. After years of feeling lost, I felt a connection I had been craving. At the time, I'd just gotten a divorce from the man I'd been with for thirteen years. This was about five years before I met John. Though it was a painful breakup, it was a relationship that taught me many things. One of them being that I wanted to learn how to communicate better with my partner. I also wanted to find someone who had similar interests. Art influenced me in many ways, and I wanted to share that passion with someone else. I wanted to share my life with someone who would understand my creative fervor.

After my previous marriage ended, I started getting into photography, which eventually led to doing it professionally, shooting for magazines and newspapers. I was good at the photography part, not so good at the administrative stuff at the time. I loved music photography and would often take photos of local bands and even did a few shows professionally from the press photo pit at larger venues.

There was a large group of people—headed by my sweet friend Sarah, a fellow artist and musician—that fundraised a camera. I started taking headshots and family photos after a while. My small business did well, and I made enough to support myself while having another part-time job.

Eventually my love for photography started fading, and it felt like an obligation due to my lack of passion for it. My health issues had also started becoming a glaring problem in my life. I started experiencing chronic back pain from a major fall down some stairs that had caused a sprain in my spine. This was also around the time that my genetic, progressive hypermobility and connective tissue disorder started manifesting. These health setbacks made holding up a camera painful, not to mention all the crouching, walking, and bending that photography entails.

Because photography had become my identity, it felt difficult to leave behind. I was known by those around me for taking photos. Each time I was introduced, it was usually as "Anni, the photographer." I loved this title and wore it with pride, but setting down my camera felt like losing a piece of myself.

I made sure John knew I understood his dilemma while also supporting his decision to try to stick it out.

There were more months of struggle, and then I started becoming sick again with something I had been struggling with on and off for years. We didn't know what it was and neither did my doctors. I was in debt from hospital stays and ambulance rides. Two doctors told me I probably had MS, but I couldn't afford an MRI, a test I needed to have for a diagnosis confirmation. When I managed to get health insurance, they wouldn't pay for the MRI, which was the one thing that could have given me an answer to my mystery nerve pain, joint looseness, and muscle weakness.

One day, it all sort of came to a head. Mystery ailments had been haunting me for a few years, with no answers in sight. My days were filled with migraines, dizziness, confusion, depression, and loss of mobility. I was becoming increasingly depressed.

My mom had spent the day with John while I was being cared for in the hospital. They were running errands and picking up my prescriptions. Little did I know they had also been to a jewelry store. John chose the perfect ring. He remembered me mentioning that I didn't much care for diamonds but loved rubies. At the store, my mom handed him two rings, one was a large ruby ring, and one was a simple, elegant vintage-style ruby ring. He chose the latter.

After my mom and John picked me up from the hospital and dropped us off at home, I was exhausted. I made myself comfortable on the couch in the living room and rested my head back. I heard him kneel down next to me and he fumbled for my hand.

I opened my eyes, and he asked me how I was feeling. I said I was tired but happy to be home with him.

"I think I have something that will make you feel better." He stood up, walking over to the coat rack on the front door.

He grabbed something from his coat and, turning around with a huge grin on his face, walked back to me.

He kneeled on the floor with both knees and, using my full legal name said, "Annalisa, will you marry me?"

I burst into tears, "Of course!"

It's not always easy, and we try not to fool ourselves by ignoring the real issues. But two things can be true at the same time. Life can be painful, and we can find something to appreciate even in the painful times.

It wasn't a romantic, champagne-fueled dinner proposal that you see in the movies. It was a down-to-earth proposal fit for us. It was meaningful and from the heart. The ring he'd chosen was perfect.

I was shocked. We hadn't talked about getting married and had even mentioned not wanting to ever get married. I'd been married once before. That relationship had lasted a total of thirteen years, four of them as a married couple. I did not want to repeat the mistakes I had made in the past. John's experiences had also left him feeling indifferent about marriage.

Little did I know, we had a little fairy in our life who was putting ideas in both of our heads. My sweet mom, who loved John so dearly, wanted to see both of us happy. John and my mom were two peas in a pod. I like to say that their hearts were painted with the same brush. John, a sweet-natured and kind person, had the same gentle demeanor my mom did. Their humor matched, as well, often using self-deprecating jokes to cope with life's difficulties.

Once, not too long before John proposed, my mom asked me, "Do you think you could ever see yourself marrying John?"

I didn't hesitate, "Definitely."

Behind the scenes, my mom's plan had started. Not long after this, she asked John the same question and his response was the same. A few days later, he asked her to take him ring shopping and you know the rest of the story!

This was a time that I appreciated my mom being nosy. I think we both just needed a nudge in the direction our hearts were already headed. As we started planning our wedding, life went on with the same obstacles of my health and our financial difficulties.

Though both of us were in low places emotionally and physically, we felt grateful every day for our shared love. Cooking meals together, taking short walks, and relaxing in our quiet backyard were oases of calm in our life.

Something that I think has held us together is our ability to see the sun through the clouds. No matter what we are facing, we understand that we are facing it together, as a team.

And we always strive to remember that every feeling is temporary and that every problem has a solution. It might not be the solution we thought it would be, but being open to the alternative paths that life presents to us has gotten us through some pretty dark days.

We are both really adept at feeling gratitude in every situation. It's not always easy, and we try not to fool ourselves by ignoring the real issues. But two things can be true at the same time. Life can be painful, and we can find something to appreciate even in the painful times. And if one of us can't find the goodness in that moment, we still hold space open for each other in the hard times.

> *No matter what we are facing, we understand that we are*
>
> *facing it together, as a team.*

An exercise we often do together during these heavy instances is to name three things we are grateful for. Even if it's small, it helps shift the focus enough to lighten the mood. Giving ourselves room to grow and make mistakes has helped our relationship immeasurably.

John has always been supportive, and I know he has sometimes felt powerless not being able to help me. My illness was affecting our ability to pay our bills. We spent a lot of time in line at food banks and I often begged the electric company to keep our lights on.

These years feel a million miles away now, but at the time, they were dark, and our good days were few and far between. On our good days, we would take slow walks in the old cemetery behind our house, followed by cooking or baking together in our tiny kitchen.

John loves baking. As a small child, he would sit on the counter at home and watch his mom bake bread. She taught him most of what he knows about baking. I had a love for cooking, and particularly loved to make stews, soups, and stir fries. We would teach each other culinary techniques and what flavors went together best.

I enjoyed watching John knead bread. It is always such a tactile experience for him. We loved doing something we called "bread tithing," distributing bread to people we loved. It was one of the things we could do that didn't cost very much.

Sometimes I did pop-up art shows, and I liked to donate a portion or all the profits to a cause that was important to me. I knew that no person was an island, and that there was always a time in each person's life in which they would need to ask for help. It's a humbling experience to be in need. John and I had both been in that position and wanted others to feel supported when they needed it.

As John's piano rebuilding projects began to dwindle, we realized we were going to have to find an alternative plan for our income. I decided to set school aside and start looking for a more secure job. My next job was at Habitat for Humanity as the office coordinator, which meant answering phones, acting as front desk customer service, and handling general office upkeep. I ended up being there for almost four years and loved it. Working at a nonprofit and helping others fit my values while giving us the income we needed.

We knew our wedding would have to be small, and neither one of us envisioned anything too fancy. It just wouldn't have fit our personalities. At first, we thought a backyard barbecue might be just our speed, but then realized that we wanted something different.

A friend of ours enjoyed planning friends' weddings as a gift, and she offered to do this for us. As John and I were trying to think of a venue for our ceremony, a lightbulb went off in my head. I told him maybe we should think about asking the community garden people if they would consider hosting our wedding there. It was the spot of our first date, and we both felt this was the perfect location, right where John's beloved pea patch was.

After getting approval from the city and paying a small fee, we started plotting out our garden spot in April of 2015. Our wedding was set for September 12th of that year.

We started out by choosing what we wanted to grow. Peas, of course, were the first to be added to the list! We planted pumpkins, cauliflowers, cabbages, sunflowers, herbs, and tomatoes. To cordon off each section, we used some old piano keys that John had in his repair supplies. We tied twine from key to key, creating dividers, and to make it easier for John to keep from trampling our growing harvest.

It became a tradition each day for us to visit our garden plot. We weeded, watered, and nourished each plant, with John able to feel the growth in his hands. We hoped that, by September, our garden would be thriving and provide a beautiful backdrop for our special day.

Conveniently, the garden had a nearby community center that rented out space for weddings and other celebrations. We reserved the venue for our reception, and I started making decorations using housing materials I purchased at the Habitat for Humanity store connected to my work office.

I made signs, built a cupcake display, and we decided to keep the centerpieces simple: mason jars with flowers from the farmers market. A lot of men might not be interested in wedding planning, but John joined in with gusto in every aspect. He helped me add hinges to the sandwich board signs I painted and built our wedding arbor using recycled materials. John even taught me how to use a jigsaw to build some of our decorations.

Our wedding was a great creative outlet for both of us, and especially for John. He was still having a hard time accepting his failing piano business, and I was very happy to see him happy. By September, our garden was beautiful. Sunflowers lined the back row of our plot, and each row of the square was a different vegetable, and a different flower.

We had invited everyone, and I do mean everyone, to our wedding. Because a friend of mine had encouraged a potluck as the answer to our small budget, that kept the food budget low and reduced any pressure to keep the guest list small.

The special day came, and it was in the low 80s. The weather cooperated with a light breeze. Our friends gathered on the grass near the garden spot. The arbor John built was at the opening of our garden bed, and I placed a light, white gauzy scarf across the top of it so it would blow in the wind as we said our vows.

A couple friends of ours played guitar and sang. John and I chose to enter the ceremony together as a symbol of all we had already overcome together. Never ones to follow the crowd, we were making our own traditions as we entered our new life, hand in hand. We were ready to create a new path and leave behind things that we no longer needed. One of those things we wanted to leave behind was living a life based on the expectations of others.

By this time, we'd shared many late night conversations and knew our spiritual beliefs were aligned. We both believe in leading with love, and treating others with kindness, empathy, and compassion. These philosophies are our moral compass.

During the ceremony, my nephew sang "our song" accompanied by our friend on guitar. During our courtship, John told me he knew what our song should be. He had chosen "Here Comes the Sun" by The Beatles. It was perfect!

Because we both found comfort in symbolism, we chose to water our garden together during the ceremony. I had found a beautiful old watering can at an antique market. We each held onto the strong, old handle of the can and I guided him over to a patch. We watered the garden together, a symbol of the growth we had already made and the growth that was ahead.

Our friend officiated for us, and we read our vows to each other. They were not traditional vows, but ones we had each written. We each started with "I promise to remain a present and nurturing partner."

Then each of us had our own individualized promises.

JOHN'S VOWS

I PROMISE TO TURN THE LIGHTS ON FOR YOU

I PROMISE TO MAKE YOU LAUGH WHEN YOU NEED IT MOST

I PROMISE TO BE YOUR EYES IN THE DARK

MY VOWS

I PROMISE TO BE YOUR EYES AND GUIDE YOU THROUGH OUR LIFE

I PROMISE TO ALWAYS DESCRIBE THE SUNSETS TO YOU

I PROMISE TO CLOSE THE KITCHEN CUPBOARDS SO
YOU DON'T HIT YOUR HEAD

AND TO HELP YOU CLEAN UP YOUR SPILLS

It was a beautiful, full-circle moment to include watering the garden in our wedding ceremony.

Our wedding day was one of the best days of
our lives, and the joy is evident on our faces.

After the ceremony, we all headed over to the venue, where our friends and family helped set up for us. Mason jars filled with flowers from the local farmers market were on each table, and the potluck dishes were laid out on a long table along one wall. A family friend of mine brewed a special beer to be served, and we had a music playlist I put together. The playlist was run by another friend of ours who was also our master of ceremonies. The dance floor was never empty, and my face hurt from smiling so much. John often says it was the best wedding he's ever been to, and I agree!

It was a treat to have so many of John's family in one place. They lived mostly near Salt Lake City, Utah. Some of his siblings couldn't make the trip out to Washington State, but it was great to have the ones who made it there.

John's cousin Katie even drove out by herself to help us set up the reception hall, and she walked around with a voice recorder to do an audio guest book. She had our friends and family record well wishes and we listened to them a couple days later as we opened gifts. It was a great memento!

John's sister Kristi, his niece Jen (Kristi's daughter), Jen's son Liam (his great-nephew), and both of John's parents made it to our wedding. Having our families meet and be in one place felt like puzzle pieces being fit together. Everyone got along great, as we were almost certain they would.

A friend's daughter was doing face painting for the kids, and we put out chalk so the children or anyone could make art on the concrete outside.

Our first dance was a song that John played for me that first week we met. We both have a quirky, sometimes dark sense of humor and the song we chose reflected that. We danced to a funny song called "Poisoning Pigeons in the Park," by Tom Lehrer.

Our day was just the celebration we envisioned, grounded in simple joys and moments of connection with people we love.

CHAPTER 8

The Steps in Between

— ANNI —

The first couple years after we got married felt like we were treading water. Sometimes we made progress upstream, but a lot of our life felt like a standstill. Now I know better; this was a time of incubation. Somewhere I read that personal growth is not linear and this was a great example of that. What looked like struggle was a slow climb and ended up being a powerful catalyst for the future we dreamed of.

In 2016, we moved to a town called Washougal, about twenty miles east of where we had been living. Our new little town had a small art community. That year, I did my first art festival. I had done art gallery showings for years, but nothing like this. I was still working at Habitat for Humanity and selling my art on the side.

For several months, John was feeling somewhat lost, not knowing what his next move would be. He did some volunteer work for Habitat for Humanity where I was working, often helping them take apart old appliances and once making centerpieces for an event. At one point he volunteered with Habitat for Humanity and helped paint and fix up a house that was connected to the piano repair school he had attended.

He tried to get piano jobs here and there, sometimes fixing up and selling pianos, but eventually came to the realization that he wanted to move on from doing piano repair. It wasn't bringing in much income and he felt creatively stifled by the repetitive nature of the work.

That September, I purchased a lathe for him for his birthday. He had talked a lot about the woodworking he had done in Utah, and I could tell it made him happy. I would look at the beautiful table in our living room and think about how much talent he had in those beautiful hands. More than anything, I just wanted John to be happy. He deserved to be happy.

I was aware of the extent to which art had saved my life over and over again. Seeing it do the same for John was all the motivation I needed to keep my eye on the ball.

The day we brought that lathe home from the hardware store felt like Christmas. He immediately headed out to the garage behind our house and set up his new toy. It brought me so much joy when he started spending hours out there. I would check in on him just to make sure he was safe.

The first bowl he made was a laminated piece. It was made using multiple pieces of wood glued together, then turned on the lathe into a bowl.

Years before, a friend and local filmmaker, Chris Martin, had made a brief documentary about me and my volunteer work in the community. Now, he asked if he could make one about John and his story for the same series.

Watch Anni's documentary via this code.

John felt like he was on the right path once again, with his first project being documented by Chris. The filming went off without a hitch and the film turned out beautifully. The very day after Chris finished recording in the wood shop, John had an accident. As he says, he "had his finger where it shouldn't be" and it caused some damage. Quite a bit!

I was inside the house at the time, and his woodshop was directly behind it. I was doing the dishes and heard a knock at the back door followed by an urgent-sounding, "Anni!" I panicked, knowing something was wrong. The moment I opened the door, I saw blood dripping down John's hand and onto the back porch. I rushed him into the bathroom to clean it up but quickly realized we needed to head to the ER.

Fortunately, eleven stitches and eight weeks later he was back to work at the lathe. This time with more knowledge of what not to do and where not to put his finger. The adaptive technique he used wasn't without its risks, but he learned a big lesson from the mishap.

When he finished the bowl, we both joked that it literally had his DNA in it. If it ever ended up on Antiques Roadshow, they'd be able to verify that it was made by him!

John's next project was a larger one. Earlier that year, an acquaintance of ours gave John an old family piano that had seen its last days and was beyond help. John spent four days meticulously taking it apart. I could tell it was a cathartic process, the last remnants of the career he'd had so much hope for. He saved the wood from the piano to make bowls out of.

The first project he chose to make from the piano wood was a large pedestal bowl, layered with different woods collected from the large instrument. The metaphor that it held was not lost on either of us. A dying musical instrument given new life by being repurposed. Much like John's story of renewal and rebirth, the wood had changed form but still lived on. When he was finished with the piece, it was donated to a silent auction for a suicide prevention fundraiser put on by a local mental health nonprofit.

☙

On August 21st, 2017, there was to be a solar eclipse. It was a huge natural event that John felt saddened not to be a part of. His love of science was evident from the books and documentaries he listened to. It was common for him to tell me about principles from all branches of science. He loved chemistry and physics most of all, but knew a bit about each discipline, including astronomy. Missing out on the eclipse was a huge disappointment for him.

I was reminded of our blind experiments from earlier in our relationship and how they brought us closer together. I wanted to somehow make this experience accessible for John. I reached out to my friends and family on Facebook, asking if anyone would be interested in participating in an event meant to make the eclipse accessible not only for John, but for blind people in general. The response was very positive, so I moved ahead

I created an online event page and reached out to the local newspaper. They wrote an article calling for poems, audio descriptions, or songs about the eclipse. On the day of the event, our little town had an eclipse party in the local town square. People gathered with their lawn chairs and special glasses.

While it was happening, the descriptions started pouring in online. I stood with John and read them to him. He was so happy to be included, experiencing it through the words of dozens of people who participated.

Though John couldn't visually experience the eclipse, I am so thankful for all the people who helped find a way for him to be included in such a once-in-a-lifetime event.

Eclipse Poem by Jenney Pauer

Saw the eclipse on a lake where the air got quiet and the world entered a blue-filtered twilight. A flock of birds shot straight up into the air and sketched a perfect Z-shape in unison but made no sound. The water was so alive with light, it shimmered and rocked as if each speck of dazzling, reflected light was a soul jumping madly into the air from the waves, waving its fists, desperate for attention. I felt it was shouting, screaming, "We are alive!" I felt it too. I was alive.

Eclipse Description by Jess Reynolds

The light outside became a warm orange and yellow tint, it was strange and like others said serene. The light reminded me as if we were all staring at each other through a tinted filter the more the moon moved over the sun, the stranger the light around us grew. Birds in the area started to flutter and fly away as if thrown off by what was going on. The shape of the eclipse eventually shrank from a crescent, to a burnt orange sliver looking as if a fire giant left its big toe nail clipping up in the sky for humans to gaze upon

Then the totality grew closer, soon we could take our glasses off in a safe manner to view this event. When it happened you could tell because it became instantly cool outside by a few degrees. The cold reminded me of a crisp fall evening as it kissed your exposed skin that prior was baking with warmth. The totality had blue hued light, with hints of silver and white dancing around the dark orb of the moon If one looked to the left and right you could see a slight glimpse of twinkling stars. I went back to staring at the glowing light dancing, trying to take in every moment of the one minute we had to look. The silver like light was dense as you looked closer to the edges of the dark moon, but flared out into a wispy like motion, resembling light paint strokes across a dark canvas.

Eclipse Poem by Tower Kathryn

Mild, wild cheddar wheel
Clean bite from upper right side
Smooth Pac-Man
Eating nothing
½ Vesica Pisces
Yellow smooth crescent moon
(It's starting to get cold)
Thumbnail clipping
Pinky nail clipping
Slowly, so slowly
It becomes a turban
Or an askance beret
On an expressionless black circle
Then a halo on a Black God
It frowns
Sometimes the little edges are sharp
Sometimes smooth and curved
Sometimes squared off
Clipping nail pinky
Clipping thumbnail
(It's starting to get warm)
Moon crescent smooth yellow
Pisces Vesica ½
Nothing eating man-pac smooth
Side left lower from bite clean
Wheel cheddar mild
Wild

Eclipse Poem by Christopher Luna

a ghostly veil is draped
over the entirety
blankets the house,
grass, & trees
stellar jays
aieennh! aiennh!
in warning
as the world goes dark
everything quiets down
& a million anxieties
suddenly recede as
a thousand gleaming crescents
fan across the patio and lawn

Eclipse Description by Heather Renee

An eclipse coming together. Three families joined together...then four, and then five. An unplanned neighborhood gathering as we all felt the strangeness in the air. Armed with cereal boxes, pin pricks, and aluminum foil or 2017 eclipse glasses, we looked to the sky. We marveled at the changing Cheshire Cat grin as the moon swallowed the sun. Science was explained while kids looked and moved on to swing under a big maple tree. A dog ran to catch a ball, oblivious to the reason for this unexpected Monday morning gathering. We all felt an odd time shifting as it slowly changed from bright morning to dusk, with a sudden chill in the air. Electronic sensor lights were triggered when the Cheshire cat grin became a tiny light bulb filament. All while the sun still seemed so bright without our special eclipse shades. Then it began its reversal, and the surreal magical day slowly rewound back into a normal Monday...until I walked under my large Maple tree and saw a hundred half moon-half sun shadows swaying on my house from leaf sun magic.

Eclipse Morning by Linda Weirather
(dedicated to John Furniss)

Our canvas concert-in-the-park chairs are ready
On the walk along our flowers.
Bees work with no attention to the cosmos,
Pink daisies that love the sun and we say the universe.
In spite of it all, this summer of our discontent,
We can settle in our chairs here without fear.
It will pass and be gone. We will enjoy the party.
We predict well, even if that can't buy an empire now,
Air cools, the bees slow a bit, but we know it will be hot after,
A sweater will do for a moment. This sliding shadow
Unites us, or distracts us, while crows and hummingbirds
Seem to speak louder, their dinosaur feet gripping harder
This gracious minute coming out of terror.

John and I celebrated the eclipse in the middle of our town square, where locals had all assembled in lawn chairs to view it. It was a great day!

Over the next couple years, we participated in art festivals, studio tours, and gallery shows. I still maintained my job at Habitat for Humanity and at one point needed to take on another job to make ends meet for us. I would work from early morning to afternoon at Habitat for Humanity, then head to a nanny job until the evening. I did this while the kids I nannied were in school, and it was extremely difficult to juggle the two jobs on top of our art pursuits. My heart yearned to create art full-time, but I had failed at it time and again and I was worried that if I ended the outside jobs it wouldn't work this time, either.

During this period, my own health became increasingly worse, despite all my attempts at changes in nutrition and exercise, and the tests I did with the doctor. The general consensus was that I had some sort of autoimmune condition, but an answer remained elusive until I was diagnosed with a hypermobility condition years later. The condition affects all the connective tissue in my body, mostly my joints and muscles. My body doesn't produce collagen correctly, and this can result in dislocations and repeated injuries such as sprains and fractures from just doing simple tasks like walking or going up stairs. Sometimes, they even happened in my sleep. There is little known about the disorder, and it has various comorbidities that cause many complications, such as allergies, blood pressure and heart rate changes, weight gain, loose joints, chronic pain, migraines, neurological issues that affect brain function, difficulty breathing, hives, dizziness and fainting, fatigue, and anxiety.

Watching John come into his own with his woodworking and art was enough fuel to keep me going. Seeing him finally reaching a level of happiness he had been searching for inspired me and made me extremely proud.

I was aware of the extent to which art had saved my life over and over again. Seeing it do the same for John was all the motivation I needed to keep my eye on the ball. The dream was to run our art business full-time, but I didn't know when I would finally be able to really live the life I dreamed of.

The opportunity would arrive sooner than I expected!

CHAPTER 9

Leap of Faith

— ANNI —

I remember the day I decided to quit my job. The feeling of wanting to move on had been with me for some time. Some of that was caused by my increasing sick days, often missing work because of chronic illness flare-ups that left me bedridden, unable to do basic daily tasks. I felt guilty, worried I was letting my coworkers down, but also knew that I was dragging my feet about what I sensed was inevitable.

At that point, I still didn't have any answers to my mystery symptoms. My hypermobility condition hadn't yet been diagnosed, and I knew that I needed to make a decision. I got home from work that day and told John I wanted to empty my retirement account and quit my job at Habitat for Humanity. I already knew I wasn't going to continue my nanny job, so my time would be one hundred percent dedicated to our new adventure.

At first, John showed concern about me quitting, worried that we wouldn't be able to get by. But, like so many things in my life, I needed to trust my intuition in this moment. I knew this was the direction we needed to take. After reassuring him that I felt confident in this decision, he jumped on board, excited about yet another adventure we would be embarking on.

We'd already had many side quests, but this now felt like the main event. My last day at my job was May 31st, 2019. That day, John was also one of the featured speakers at a sold-out engagement akin to a TED Talk. He had been practicing for a couple months and would be sharing his story with a theater packed with 340 people.

As John stood on the stage wearing jeans and a black blazer, a spotlight shone on him. He was surrounded by a dark stage. I remember thinking how handsome he looked.

Those moments of sharing my art with John fostered a unique intimacy I've never had with anyone else.

Photo by Rachel Konsella.

He came out on stage saying, "I must say, you are all looking wonderful."

A laugh erupted from the audience. John spent the next thirteen minutes telling the story of his suicide attempt, his battle with hard drugs, and his journey into woodworking.

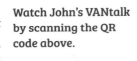

Watch John's VANtalk by scanning the QR code above.

I sat in the third row with tears in my eyes for most of his talk. I could barely see him through my tears, but I had memorized the talk, just as he had. We had spent many late nights writing it together, rehearsing over and over to make sure it was timed just right.

I was bursting with pride as I listened to my husband speak in public. He had been my hero all these years and this felt like the beginning of something big. Everything felt like it was lining up, and my heart soared with the providence of what was to come.

That summer, we started doing more art festivals and had some really successful experiences. It was always hard to guess if the events we signed up for would be worth the time and energy. We loved them because we got to meet a lot of people, and would encourage people to bring their dogs to visit us. It became a tradition for people to get their dog's photo taken with John.

John and I soon started collaborating on art projects together. It started out one day when John brought in a bowl that had cracked while he was making it.

"Can you do anything with this?" he asked.

"Heck, yeah!" I was excited to have a creative problem to solve.

This bowl had multiple cracks in it. I painted it blue with a dragonfly. It was the start of what John calls his "Oops, I mean ta-da!" projects. Since then, I've painted his oops pieces with honeybees, butterflies, mushrooms, frogs, and more dragonflies.

Eventually, I started playing around more and more with tactile art. I wasn't very familiar with sculpting at this point but have never been one to shy away from trying something new. Even if I'm not good at it, if it's fun, I'll give it a go.

Here, we're packing up several of John's pieces before a trip to Utah, where John is from. He wanted to show them off to his family!

On one project, I turned one of my paintings into a sculpture. John made the base, and I sculpted a whale with a hot-air balloon attached to the top of it. It was satisfying that John was finally able to really experience my art in a tactile way.

I watched as his hands explored the textures and contours of the piece. His face lit up as he realized what the piece was, the original painting was based on an idea he came up with, so he recognized it immediately.

Those moments of sharing my art with John fostered a unique intimacy I've never had with anyone else.

We did as many art shows and bazaars as we could physically handle. Then, in July of 2019, I experienced a major setback when one of my dearest friends, Kelly Keigwin, died after a long struggle with cancer. Her art influenced me greatly and we'd been friends for many years. She would post photos of hearts on her social media that she found randomly in public and would frequently put hearts in her artwork.

The loss of Kelly impacted me deeply. I sat with her at her bedside, holding her hand as she passed on. I was no stranger to grief. When I was sixteen years old, I lost my grandmother in much the same way, holding her hand as she died from cancer. When I was ten, I lost my baby sister to SIDS. The grief I felt after Kelly died triggered a deep sadness in me and put me in a deep depression. I missed my friend every day but still felt the fire to create, this time using my art to process the grief.

About a week after Kelly died, John and I were filmed for an art special on our local PBS channel. The special was called "Oregon Art Beat." On the episode, I am in the process of painting a portrait of Kelly, my grief still very apparent. I didn't think I would sell the painting until a social worker inquired about buying it to put in her office to give her clients peace. It felt so good knowing that Kelly's presence would be comforting people, much like she did when she was alive.

That fall, John and I started talking about how we were going to make ends meet in February of the coming year. It's very common for artists to struggle following the holidays because of the lack of events or festivals. Inspired by my friend Kelly's love of hearts, we came up with the idea to put on an art festival around Valentine's Day. We called it Washougal Love Fest. I was looking forward to getting back into event organizing.

That was also the year that John decided he wanted to apply for a pardon for his felony. We both knew it would be a long process, but it had been weighing on John and he wanted to be free from the stigma it carried. It had been eighteen years since his arrest and fourteen years since he got off probation. I told him I would help him with the process. To begin, I helped him gather the reference letters he would need. I also helped him fill out the paperwork for the state of Colorado. We told his story and all he'd overcome. I even sent in photos of his creations. We sent it by certified mail and held our breath.

The application process for a pardon is a pretty involved one, and it requires the coordination of multiple parties. After all his paperwork was mailed in, the paperwork had to be processed and the information verified. Then, the director convened with the Executive Clemency Advisory Board, who would review the materials and forward their recommendations to the state governor. Once submitted, the governor takes the application under advisement (which doesn't necessarily mean it will be quickly reviewed). If clemency is granted, the governor's office notifies the legislature, and then the applicant is notified of the decision.

In December of that year, John received a phone call from the Colorado courthouse. He had gotten his pardon approved by the governor. It was a few days before Christmas, so it felt like the best present he could have asked for! He remembers fondly how excited the woman on the phone sounded for him.

Unfortunately, my health continued to decline, and by Christmas, I became very ill. The holiday art bazaars were particularly awful for me, since I had migraines and muscle weakness at most of them. I tried to smile my way through them, but was fading with each one. I was spending more and more time in bed and planned most of our upcoming festival from there. I had a few other people helping me with things like coordinating volunteers and performance art.

I had a surgery scheduled for after the festival in February, but I had to somehow push through to make it until then. We still had bills to pay, and I didn't want to disappoint anyone by canceling the Love Fest. We had a lot of artists depending on us for their income, too!

CHAPTER 10

Such Great Heights

JOHN

When we started organizing an art festival in 2019, we had no way to know that it would be our final public event. Anni took the lead arranging most of the details, and I provided her with emotional support throughout the process. Whenever possible, I assisted by making phone calls where needed. Anni's determination was further bolstered by the support of our friends who helped distribute posters and coordinated volunteers for the event day. It was heartwarming to witness the collaboration and effort put in by everyone involved in making the art festival a memorable success.

It went from an idea, just a thought, to a reality in about three months. We called it "Love Fest" and we held the event in February of 2020. The idea was to give artists an opportunity to create income during a time when art sales are historically low. Between Christmas and Summer, there aren't many festivals or avenues for artists to make a living.

Anni was having more mobility and chronic health issues, and she was waiting for an upcoming surgery. It was another time in our life that our friends and family were there for us. Giving back to our community was an easy way for us to show our gratitude.

The day arrived for Love Fest. There were forty vendors, mostly artists from the local community. We had painters, ceramists, fiber artists, and woodworkers. There was a roving magician doing tricks for the attendees and we even invited a troupe of people who dressed up as *Star Wars* stormtroopers. There was a performance artist dressed as a statue and a table where people could share their love stories with a documentarian. There was also a table run by the library with children's crafts, and the local coffee shop gave away free coffee. The day was more than we could

The world of social media was new to both of us. There is no guide telling you how to handle all that comes with sudden "fame."

Love Fest 2020 was full of positivity and friendship and community. The support it received was unbelievable.

have imagined. It encompassed all things love and community. In the end, nearly 1,500 people attended.

Little did we know that this would be the very last public art event that Anni and I would do together. In March of 2020, the world shut down. That year we had multiple art festivals scheduled, and they were going to be our main source of income.

When the pandemic hit, every event we signed up for was canceled and we felt our dreams were disappearing like smoke in the wind. Feeling panicked, we started brainstorming for other ways we could survive. Anni started applying for artist grants and we were fortunate enough to qualify for a couple. Then, a friend of ours suggested that we start posting on TikTok. We laughed, thinking it was just an app for teenagers to dance and make music on, not a place for a couple of middle-aged artists!

But it turned out to be the best advice we could possibly have received. We began by posting videos called "Cooking with the Lights Out," a series about baking and cooking. With Anni's love of cooking and my love of baking, it was the perfect combo.

It took off, to say the least! Our videos started going viral, and pretty soon people were asking about buying our art. We started selling to people all over the country.

I hate to say it, but that year was a blessing in disguise for us. I know it was a painful time for many businesses, so we recognize that we were among the lucky ones. People were dying and losing family members. It filled us with guilt that our lives took an upward turn while so many others took a turn for the worse. But the truth was that people were stuck at home, and the growth in online shopping was a trend that tilted in our favor. What's more, we started realizing that our videos were bringing joy to people in a difficult time.

It was a mixed bag, knowing the world was experiencing such a huge calamitous change and widespread economic insecurity. Finding the good during those days helped our mental health, as well.

Pretty soon we started sharing my story and all the challenges I'd overcome. Emails, messages, and comments came pouring in from people all over the world, telling us about their struggles with mental health and disability.

Before the advent of COVID-19, we'd been doing talks in high schools, and Anni began to notice that teachers would often ask students, "Turn off your TikTok." It made us realize that the app would be a great place to reach teens during the pandemic. Since our school talks had also been canceled, this was a great way to reach the kids.

It's fair to say that 2020 changed our lives. It was a mixed bag, knowing the world was experiencing such a huge calamitous change and widespread economic insecurity. Finding the good during those days helped our mental health, as well. Anni was able to focus on her art and her love of videography. She was the producer, director, videographer, and editor. I joke that I just stand there and look pretty. But in all seriousness, it was a nice way for us both to share our gifts and spend time together. It strengthened our relationship in new ways.

One of our popular segments is Cooking with the Lights Out, in which John shows off his cooking skills while answering questions from our followers.

From then on, our social media community grew and grew. With Anni running things behind the scenes and me in front of the camera, we once again made a great team. I shared about woodworking, mental health struggles, baking, blindness, and my favorite—I had the opportunity to share my silliness.

We started a few different video series, including one in which I come in the back door from the woodshop with a piece newly created on the lathe. Then, I trade the piece with Anni for some food. This bit became a crowd favorite. Millions and millions of views later, we started sharing more about our marriage and making videos about our art collaborations.

The world of social media was new to both of us. There is no guide telling you how to handle all that comes with sudden "fame." After a while, we would be recognized in public. People would stop and tell us how much they loved our videos. This was so surreal! We still aren't quite used to it, but always welcome a hello. Today we have over two million followers across our social media platforms. It's still hard to wrap our heads around. Social media has been an impactful tool for us to reach others. It's allowed us not only to make a living selling our art, but to share our messages about finding purpose, creating connection, and overcoming the stigma of mental illness. I never in a million years imagined that I would be sharing my most intimate trauma with millions of people around the world.

Another aspect of a big social media following is moderating the inevitable negative comments. That's the reality of sharing our life publicly. Anni was bearing the brunt of this because she runs all our online platforms. She would come to me crying some days about the horrible things being said. She deleted and blocked as many as she could, but some days I reminded her it was okay to take a break and focus on other things.

Nowadays, the word filters are stronger and so is our skin. We've learned to not let the negative comments get to us as much. Those people, much like the bullies I encountered in childhood, are hurting and use their pain to wound others. It's unfortunate but it's also not our job to try to change their minds.

We choose to focus on the goodness that we are blessed to be surrounded by from our online community.

We started forming friendships with other content creators and found kinship in the disability community. I encouraged Anni to start sharing a little more about her chronic illness and soon others shared their experiences with chronic illness as well. Having a disability can be lonely and isolating. When we hear others talking about the unpleasant side of social media, we like to remind them of the benefits. When someone is homebound, for instance with a disability, social media gives them connection. It's an accessible way to socialize with others and create community. It allows people to connect with a diverse community of people who share similar experiences, interests, and challenges. This sense of camaraderie can be incredibly comforting. There is a large blind community online. Through adaptive technology and other accessible things such as alt text (a built-in function that describes images), and audio description, the internet has become a much more habitable place for people who are visually impaired.

We both firmly believe that awareness about blindness and disability is a powerful antidote to ignorance.

Accessible technology breaks down physical barriers for people too. It enables them to engage in conversations and events regardless of whether that person can speak, see, hear, or walk. People can easily advocate for disability rights on a global scale and raise awareness on issues faced by people with disabilities. Harnessing the power of social media gives people access to information, resources, and vital support networks.

Soon news outlets started reaching out, wanting to do segments on me and my story. BuzzFeed, Upworthy, CBS, *People* magazine, NBC, ABC, the list goes on. We were awestruck at the coverage. It was amazing to realize my message was reaching millions and millions of people.

Was this our life now?

We both knew that in order to help change the world even a little, we'd need to put ourselves out there. We both firmly believe that awareness about blindness and disability is a powerful antidote to ignorance.

The same could be said for any misunderstood demographic. When society embraces education and understanding, misconceptions and prejudice begin to dissolve.

Increased knowledge not only encourages others to see beyond physical limitations but also helps create environments where individuals with disabilities can survive (and thrive) and contribute their unique perspectives.

For many years after my suicide attempt, I had a dream to become an inspirational speaker. Starting in my early 20s I began thinking of sharing my story with others. One day, when I was around 21, I was sitting talking with my then-girlfriend Kathi and my friend Deborah.

Kathi said to me, "John, have you thought about writing a book about your life?"

Deborah responded, "I think he needs to do a lot more living first."

I agreed with her. I hadn't yet healed enough or done enough living.

When Anni and I were asked to write this book, that moment with Deborah was the first thing I thought of. I knew it was finally time.

CHAPTER 11

Life Is but a Dream

ANNI

Our life now is incredibly different than we could've imagined just a few years ago. That is not to say we are without our struggles. Both John and I still must wrestle with our mental health and various health issues.

I am really stubborn, ask those closest to me. John knows this more than anyone because he, too, is a very stubborn person. I've spent the last dozen years in denial about my conditions, often daydreaming about when I would be "whole" again. For about two years, I was feeling better but found out recently my efforts with daily yoga and extreme nutrition changes actually made my conditions worse in the end. Because of the way the collagen is produced in my body, my joints are weak, and I can easily injure myself. Each person that has this condition is different, but for me, I have to be careful when exercising, lifting, standing, or walking long distances.

In 2021, I severely injured my neck while doing yoga and ended up in the hospital. They did an MRI of my neck and upper spine, finding some damage that was progressive and had probably been happening gradually over years. After I came home from the hospital, I was unable to even walk from the bedroom to the living room. John had to take on a short-term caregiving role for me, cooking, cleaning, and helping me shower and get to the bathroom. I had to start using a walker, which I named "Sheila" and decorated with stickers. It was a way for me to accept this new mobility aid.

One night, after John tripped over "Sheila," I was embarrassed and cried. I asked John, "Are there classes like the ones you go to where I learn how to accept that I'm disabled?" He said it took him years to accept that his disability is permanent. Though mine has progressively gotten worse over the last couple years, I held onto hope that I would someday be athletic and agile.

Through all our struggles, we strive to create a happy life together.

My reality is that I have many mental and physical challenges that I'm trying to embrace so I can adapt and move forward. I have neurological issues, anxiety disorder, fibromyalgia, osteoarthritis, degenerative bone disease, and lordosis (I now jokingly call it Lord of the Osis). And now I had a new hypermobility diagnosis, which was the most difficult of all of them.

I have preached for many years that disability isn't a bad word. I've been a cheerleader for John and a disability advocate. I've never accepted that I, too, have several disabilities. People have assumed because John has a visible disability that I should be the one caring for him. "Oh, it's so nice he has you to take care of him."

But John said he has felt guilty for so long that I suffer silently with invisible disabilities.

I'm working to embrace my challenges and use the tools that are available to me. Having a spouse who understands what it's like grieving the loss of a "whole" body and accepting a new reality is priceless.

I think the hardest aspect of all this, besides losing my mobility, is the weight gain that has come with my lack of activity. I can't move as often as I'd like to, so I've gained about 60 pounds in the last three years. As someone who has struggled for most of my life with body dysmorphia and general insecurity, this has been very difficult—especially since I live a very public life in front of millions of people on the internet.

I am fortunate to have an understanding, empathetic spouse who loves me regardless of my physical appearance. Because John has his own disabilities, he knows this can often mean abilities change over time. Needs can change, and this means being able to shift course and find things that work. We now have new things in our house that we didn't think we'd need until older age: a shower chair, walker, canes, a stool for doing the dishes.

This process I've gone through has brought us even closer. I am still working on acceptance and grieving over the loss of my mobility and changes to my physical appearance. I am at a point in my life where I can accept what is happening and use the tools available to me or I can live in denial, fight it, and make things harder on both of us. I'm taking a page out of John's book and choosing to accept myself. I am lucky to be facing a disability with a supportive spouse. He's been in my position and uses patience, empathy, and kindness to help me navigate this difficult change.

Through all our struggles, we strive to create a happy life together. Our life is pretty simple, social media "fame" aside. On an average day, we wake up and eat breakfast and take care of our pup. Then, we each do our physical therapy (treadmill and recumbent bike). After that, John gets dressed and goes out to the woodshop for the day.

I stay in the house and work on answering emails, editing videos for social media and creating posts, and doing general admin work. Some days, I'm photographing products for our store, uploading them, or working on our website or newsletter. Also depending on the day, I'm fulfilling orders by packaging them up, weighing them and making labels, and then taking them to the post office.

I am at a point in my life where I can accept what is happening and use the tools available to me or I can live in denial, fight it, and make things harder on both of us.

My favorite days are the ones where I get to work on my art.

John comes in for lunch sometimes, but usually, I meet him at the door, and he takes it out to his shop so he doesn't get sawdust in the house— which is his choice! I don't mind sweeping it up.

I like to visit him in his shop to check in on him, and sometimes we make videos for our social media.

By my side most days as I work is Pickle, our "furry intern," as we call him. He came to us in August of 2013, a wonderful, unexpected surprise in our lives. My friend Jenney called me frantically looking for someone to take in a stray dog she had found chasing squirrels in her neighborhood. The Humane Society was closed, and she couldn't take him in because of other obligations. This was a friend well-known for rescuing animals, and I told her I would love to help.

She came to our house within minutes, and we met her out in the driveway. Jenney placed the little dog into my arms, and it was instant

Pickle doesn't always look so angry, but he gets a bit camera shy!

love. He was a terrier mix, with soft, blonde-colored hair and short ears. I felt his wiggly body melt into mine, and my heart practically exploded.

We took him inside to inspect him a little closer. He was covered in fleas, emaciated, and hadn't been neutered. He also hadn't had a bath in a long time.

John turned to me and asked, "What do you think his name is?"

Without hesitation, I responded, "His name is Pickle. I'm not sure how I know that, but that's his name."

John laughed and said, "I believe you're right!"

The next day I called the Humane Society to report him, and they told me if the owners didn't come forward within thirty days, we could keep him. They were grateful we were willing to "foster" him in the meantime. We did our due diligence on social media to find his owners, but John and I both knew there probably was nobody looking for him. He showed signs of neglect, which meant he had probably been on the street for a while.

When we fed him, he timidly waited until I told him it was okay. He constantly looked around to make sure it was safe to eat. It broke our hearts, as it seemed likely he had been underfed and possibly mistreated.

During those thirty days we showered him with love, and he started integrating into our lives. The deadline came and I received a phone call from my mom congratulating us. He was officially part of our family and still is ten years later! We jokingly call him our fur kid.

The three of us live a fairly quiet life. On our days off, John and I like to go on walks on our favorite trails or have lunch at a nearby restaurant. We also enjoy doing crossword puzzles together, watching our favorite shows and movies, cooking, and baking. Above all, we try to be the peace for each other that we were so often lacking in our lives, and to hold the space for us to each be ourselves. So, while our life might be simple, it is good.

Our platform has become a safe place for us and for the millions that follow our pages. Our online space has become a way to share awareness about blindness, disabilities, mental health, and art. When we decided to start sharing about the small joys of our lives, and then the deeper struggles we face, little did we know that we were building a community. The people we've met and the lives we've touched have done as much for us as they say we've done for them, if not more. I hope this book we've written comes through as an expression of the love we share with each other and with the world.

CHAPTER 12

If You Can't See, Imagine

JOHN

Working in my woodshop has taught me some very valuable lessons.

Lesson Number One: Don't put your finger there.

The same can be said for many things in life. Using mindfulness both in the woodshop and out not only keeps me safe, but it reminds me to slow down and enjoy the journey I'm on. This brings me to my next point.

Lesson Number Two: Be patient.

When I drop something, it can take me upwards of an hour to find it. Now, I could ask for help, but my rock-hard stubbornness prevents me from doing this a lot of the time. I will search on my hands and knees, sometimes for what feels like an eternity. I'm certain I have a woodshop gremlin that either kicks things under my benches or steals my things. I'm sure he has a belt with a few of my tools on it, too. In my hours spent trying to find these elusive objects, I have learned to be patient. I have to be if I want to keep my sanity.

Much like mindfulness, patience translates to most things I do in life. If I want a ride somewhere, I need to surrender to the fact that I will be relying on someone else to get me there. Whether that is waiting for the city bus at the bus stop, getting a ride from my wife, or reserving a taxi, I simply have to wait. That is, unless I'm walking somewhere, and even then I need to be aware and alert always of every passing car and steep curb. Sometimes I have to memorize new paths or remember landmarks.

After I bashed my face the first few times or broke a glass or spilled a cup, I learned that I had a higher chance of avoiding these with just a dash

The woodshop is more than just a workspace for me, it's a classroom that imparts valuable life lessons that resonate far beyond the feel of sawdust.

of patience. Slowing down is the way to go. That philosophy has also helped me go with the flow and read what the Universe has to show me.

Embracing patience has not only empowered me to overcome obstacles, but it has also opened doors to endless possibilities and a deeper appreciation for beauty in life beyond sight.

With blindness, I have had to learn new ways to listen to my surroundings using other senses. I have learned to use new assistive technology, not always well, but well enough that it has opened up a new world for me.

One of my favorite quotes about patience is often attributed to Bruce Lee: "Patience is not passive, on the contrary it is concentrated strength."

It's taken me many years to harness the power of slowing down. I rely on my inner calm to carefully explore and adapt to new environments. Embracing patience has not only empowered me to overcome obstacles, but it has also opened doors to endless possibilities and a deeper appreciation for beauty in life beyond sight.

It is through patience that I have discovered the strength to embrace my journey as a blind individual with resilience and optimism.

Lesson Number Three: Find joy in life.

There have been many times in my life where I could have gotten mad or irritated with myself. For instance, once I tripped over a lawn mower in our yard (that I had left there) and did some midair acrobatics over the top of it like a hero in an action movie. Afterward, I laid on the ground laughing at the thought of my unintentional stunt!

In another instance I was crossing a very large street in Salt Lake City, probably about eight lanes wide. I had just enough time to get across the street, and that was if I was in good working order. At the time, I was not. I had injured my right ankle, so I wore one of those walking boot contraptions that you have to strap to your leg with Velcro. I had a crutch under my right arm, and I had my cane in my left hand, so I had to work out a system where I swung the cane as I was using the crutch. I was about halfway across the street, and the light changed. There was no beeper! I knew the light had changed because I heard all the people start to go, so I picked up my foot and ran the rest of the way across the road with my big boot and my crutch. When I finally got to the other side, the image of me running across the street went through my mind, and I had a good laugh!

Being able to laugh at myself has gotten me through some pretty tough situations. Having a good attitude is not always easy for me, but it's been essential in surviving my blindness. Humor has become an invaluable companion for me in my everyday life. Laughter helps me break down barriers and connect with others in a unique way. I use playful banter and self-deprecating humor about how I navigate my surroundings. My witty comebacks about misconceptions people may have regarding blindness relieves any awkwardness someone might have around me. Humor has allowed me to approach situations with a lighthearted perspective. It not only lightens the weight of challenges I face, but also helps me build strong relationships with friends and family, who've come to expect my goofy jokes, and strangers I meet, which buoys daily life.

Lesson Number Four: Perseverance.

The journey of navigating the world without sight has presented its fair share of challenges, but with each obstacle, I have discovered the strength to persist and adapt. It's not all puppies and rainbows everyday, if I'm being realistic. Some days it's about accepting my limits and finding creative paths to accomplish what I need or want to get done. Sometimes, regularly doing the job would be far too dangerous for me, or I feel unsafe using a particular type of tool. You can usually find another way to complete the same step, even though it might take more elbow grease, or extra work. I don't mind either one, since they ensure that I can keep all ten fingers.

The key to my perseverance lies in embracing the belief that limitations are merely opportunities for creative problem-solving. That doesn't mean that there aren't days I turn the air blue in my shop with some choice words uttered over a broken piece. I m no angel, and I'm flawed just like anyone else. Putting these philosophies into practice is also part of the challenge. Believing them and practicing them are two different stories. But I have a choice in those moments. I have come to understand that setbacks are stepping stones toward growth. The moments of frustration and doubt only serve to fuel my resolve to push forward and prove to myself and others that blindness does not define my potential.

Once, I was walking to a friend's house in my old town of Craig. I was crossing over a small bridge that spanned a stream not much wider than a couple lanes of traffic. As I was passing over the bridge, I tried switching my cane to my left hand so I could follow the guard rails on my right. I fumbled the pass and down went my cane over the bridge! My cane slipped through my hand, and I leaned slightly over to try to catch it. The handle string brushed my fingers, and I heard a splash down in the water below. It was springtime so the water was running high—no way was I ever going to get it back.

I stood there for a few seconds wondering what I was going to do. I came up with the idea to follow the gutter with my foot. I needed something to remind me where I was in relation to my surroundings and the gutter was perfect. My friend's house was a little ways down and around the corner so I didn't need to cross any streets.

I know Craig so well and have such a detailed visual image of every square inch of that town that I am able to navigate rather easily using those memories. Sadly, I didn't have a spare cane at home, so my mom ordered one for me and I had to wait for it to arrive. In the meantime, I walked all over town with my friends. I used their voices and the sounds of their footsteps as a guide. I had a near picture-perfect memory of the layout of Craig, so most places we went I didn't need guidance.

The lost cane taught me that if I can't do something one way, I can find another way of doing it. Creativity isn't just saved for my woodshop. It spills over into everything I do in life.

Just as I measure twice (or thrice!) and cut once in the woodshop, I find myself applying the same methodology when tackling challenges in my personal and professional life. The ability to visualize and plan a project before taking action has taught me to approach goals with a clear vision in my mind, ensuring better outcomes and avoiding unnecessary mistakes. The satisfaction of turning raw materials into something beautiful in the woodshop instills a sense of accomplishment that motivates me to pursue greatness in other aspects of my life. The woodshop is more than just a workspace for me, it's a classroom that imparts valuable life lessons that resonate far beyond the feel of sawdust.

Imagination is one of the things that makes this world the complex, wonderful place that it is. Every single invention, song, and idea that ever came to pass began in someone's imagination. I like to say that brilliance is born in an instant. Every extraordinary idea, every groundbreaking philosophy or invention is a convergence of the events, experiences, knowledge, wisdom, and chance that caused that thing to be born into the world—to affect it for good or for ill forevermore.

Another of my favorite quotes is from Martin Luther King Jr. He said, "If you can't fly, then run. If you can't run, then walk. If you can't walk, then crawl."

And I say, if you can't see, imagine.

Acknowledgments

John's Acknowledgments

I want to start by acknowledging the love of my life, Anni, a.k.a. HoneyBee. She is my biggest fan, greatest supporter, and my life's companion. I am so blessed to have found her. This book literally would not exist without her. This book is like a recipe, though it's about my life. She did most of the writing. I provided a lot of the raw ingredients, and she baked the cake. She has helped me through some of the most difficult times as I was trying to find myself and find my place in the world. She has always encouraged me to follow the path that feels right, and I think she knows me better than I know myself. Our meeting was definitely arranged by the Cosmos (you may call it Divinity, God, or Spirit). There is no other way to explain how we found such a perfect match to each other. I truly believe that the Universe spent years gathering all the cast of characters together, finding the right location, and getting the background created and the props in the sets just right. The Cosmos said, "Action!" and our story began.

I also want to send out a big thank-you above to Bud. I know without any doubt or question that, without Bud's companionship and support, I would not be here today. He also taught me a lot of things about life and gave me a love and desire to come up here to Washington state, which is the best thing I have ever done. Bud left this earthly plane in December of 2011, but he will never leave my heart.

A very big thanks to my best friend and mentor, Chris Hathaway. Without his teachings, I would never have become The Blind Woodsman, and honestly, I have no idea what I would've done with my life. Until I started the woodworking class at the school for the blind in Salt Lake City, I did not know what I was capable of. There were many years between learning to woodwork and becoming a professional woodworker, but they were some of the best times of my life.

I am eternally grateful to my Momma and Papa. They taught me to always be honest, kind, and stay dedicated to the path that I am on. They taught me to be true to my values, and stand up for what I believe in. They were always by my side, even through the hard times and those times that I wanted to distance myself from everyone so that I could forge my own path. Even if that was not a very good path, they never abandoned or shunned me for my actions. They were always there to pick me up when I fell down and help me get back on my feet again. I would not be alive if it weren't for their love and help, and I most certainly would not be the man that I am today. I love them both with all my heart and soul, and always will.

I am grateful for the love of all my siblings. We are all so different, and we may be in different states, but I still feel connected through our memories and love.

I am forever grateful to my sister Kellie. She is the one who saved my life on April 10th, 1998. When she saved my life that day, she helped me be reborn into the person I am today. Over the years, I have come to view that day as my second birthday, and I would never have had that without her.

Thank you to my friend Deborah Brown. About 22 years ago, someone said that I should have a book written about me. Deborah shook her head and told me I needed to do some more living first. That was the very first thing I thought of when we started to write this book. I will never forget you, Deborah. You've been a good friend.

And thank you to my Aunt Laurie and Uncle Ray. They took me in many times during my couch-surfing days. If I ever needed groceries or a place to stay, they were there for me, no questions asked.

Anni's Acknowledgments

Once I wrote a list. On that list were traits, things like hands of an artist, kindness, a keen wit and a compassionate heart. I wrote this wish list in 2010, a year and a half before I met John. It didn't feel like an accident that the day we met felt written in pen, written with the most permanent ink. I knew on our first date that we were destined for the kind of rare love I dreamed of. And though our life together has been full of some painful moments, the deep bond we've formed is worth the uphill battles. John is my love, my heart, my life. Don't get me wrong, I am my own woman and always have been. But with him, I am a queen, and he never fails to help me straighten my crown. Thank you, babe. Without you, my life is just written in pencil.

I'm so grateful for my family. We may not be perfect, but our imperfections have only strengthened the bonds that hold us together. We've faced and overcome great hardships, proving that our love and support for each other can conquer any challenge. Thank you for being supportive in your various ways, for your unwavering love, and for standing by me in both joy and sorrow. I am truly blessed to have such a loving and resilient family.

John and I both want to thank Dave Miller. This book would not have happened without our immediate connection with him. When we met over a video call one day, I knew this book was meant to happen. Thank you for your gentle guidance, your patience, and for really seeing us.

We'd like to thank all our editors: managing editor Gretchen Bacon, book editor Joseph Borden, and editor Philip Turner. You helped us craft our story into a beautiful text that we will forever treasure.

Thanks, also, to our awesome PR director at Fox Chapel, Elizabeth Martins! And thank you to the rest of the staff at Fox Chapel!

And, finally, a HUGE thank you to our friends, Vancouver/Washougal community members, and all of our online social media community for supporting our dreams in so many ways. We love all of you!

Blindness Education

In understanding and practicing blindness etiquette, it's important to appreciate the array of training, technology, and mobility aids available to those with visual impairments. In the world of Orientation and Mobility (O&M) training, the goal is to empower individuals to master the essential skills for safe and independent travel in their homes and communities.

These skills aren't just about getting from point A to point B; they're the keys to unlocking every aspect of daily life. O&M instructors play a pivotal role as guides, not only in teaching navigation techniques but in helping people optimize their use of all available senses. It's a process that goes beyond physical movement—it's about enhancing one's spatial awareness and cultivating a profound connection to the surrounding environment.

The following information isn't comprehensive, but this is a great place to start learning about blindness if it's new for you.

Essential Tools That Blind People Might Use

- **Long Cane:** Serves to provide detection and information about the immediate environment. It allows the user to know about objects in the path of travel, changes in the surface of travel, and the integrity of the surface. Canes come in a variety of lengths and with a variety of tips.
- **Monocular:** A monocular is a miniature, low-powered telescope or spotting scope which you hold in your hand like a binocular but use with one eye like a telescope. It is a low-vision device used to read near (price tags) and far (street signs).
- **Tactile Maps:** Tactile maps are designed to be read by touch. They help students build a "cognitive map" of an area or remember the steps on a route they are learning to travel.
- **Screen Readers:** Screen readers are software programs that allow blind or visually impaired users to read the text that is displayed on the computer or smartphone screen with a speech synthesizer or braille display.
- **Speech to Text Programs:** - By utilizing screen readers or specialized software such as Speechify that converts written text into spoken words,

allowing users to listen to and interact with digital content, such as websites, documents, and messages.

- **Smartphone:** Most smartphones have accessibility settings to navigate and use email, text, social media, streaming platforms, and make most websites accessible.
- **Audio Description:** Most streaming platforms offer a description setting for TV shows or movies, but not all have them. It provides narration for scenes that don't have dialogue, describes body language, scenery, costumes, or appearances.
- **Mobile Apps:** Apps like Be My Eyes or Seeing AI offer descriptions of the world around you using either crowdsourced information or artificial intelligence.
- **Magnifiers:** Handheld video or screen magnifiers enlarge things to make them easier for low-vision individuals to see.
- **Audio Books:** The Library of Congress has a very large collection of audiobooks to download for free available to blind or print-disabled individuals. A print disability is a difficulty or inability to read printed material due to a perceptual, physical, or visual disability (such as Parkinson's, MS, etc.).
- **Braille:** Braille is a system of raised dots that can be read with the fingers by people who are blind or who have low vision.
- **Guide Dogs:** Dog guides are highly trained animals that provide people who are blind or visually impaired with enhanced mobility, companionship, the opportunity to conquer barriers, and increased independence.
- **Talking Household Items:** Everyday objects that provide information audibly, such as clocks, blood pressure machines, tape measures, and much more.

Basic Blindness Etiquette

- It's important to ask someone before you guide them. Respect their personal space, and do not touch them without permission. Inquire if the person needs assistance first, and if they would like you to guide them, you can offer your elbow for them to lightly hold as you walk.
- Introduce yourself by name.
- Let them know when you are leaving the conversation so they are not left speaking to themselves!
- Be specific in your verbal directions. Words such as "over there" or "that way" are not helpful to most people who are blind. Using degrees or clock directions such as clock positions, clockwise, counterclockwise, or "left" and "right" are preferred.
- Use everyday language. Don't avoid words like "see" or "look."
- Address someone by name so they know you are speaking to them.
- Don't assume someone needs help, but if they appear to be struggling, offer help.
- Do not leave doors ajar. Close them or open them fully.
- Describe, describe, describe. For example, if you are watching a movie that doesn't have audio description, offer to describe scenery, clothing, or read captions.
- Speak in a normal tone; there's no need to amplify your voice unless they are also hearing impaired.
- Address the person directly, do not speak through their guide, friend, or family.
- Don't turn blindness into a game. For example, don't make someone guess your voice. Pranks are not generally welcome; they can be dangerous.
- Never pet a working guide dog without permission, and always ask for permission to interact with them.
- Be yourself! Interacting in a new environment can be awkward for some people, but it's okay to make mistakes as long as you are willing to learn.

Thanks to Dani Kala from Washington State School for the Blind for helping us compile information for this section.